D0127044

Critical Thinking: Building the Basics

SECOND EDITION

Timothy L. Walter
Oakland Community College

Glenn M. Knudsvig
University of Michigan

Donald E. P. Smith
University of Michigan

THOMSON

WADSWORTH

Australia • Canada • Mexico • Singapore • Spain
United Kingdom • United States

College Success Editor: *Annie Mitchell*
Assistant Editor: *Kirsten Markson*
Technology Project Manager: *Barry Connolly*
Project Manager, Editorial Production: *Paula Berman*
Print/Media Buyer: *Lisabeth Martin*
Permissions Editor: *Joohee Lee*

Production Service: *G&S Typesetters, Inc.*
Copy Editor: *G&S Editors*
Cover Designer: *Bill Stanton*
Cover Image: © *Pete Turner, GettyImages, The Image Bank*
Compositor: *G&S Typesetters, Inc.*
Text and Cover Printer: *Webcom Limited*

COPYRIGHT © 2003 Wadsworth, a division of Thomson Learning, Inc. Thomson Learning™ is a trademark used herein under license.

ALL RIGHTS RESERVED. No part of this work covered by the copyright hereon may be reproduced or used in any form or by any means—graphic, electronic, or mechanical, including but not limited to photocopying, recording, taping, Web distribution, information networks, or information storage and retrieval systems—without the written permission of the publisher.

Printed in Canada
4 5 6 7 06 05

For more information about our products, contact us at:

Thomson Learning Academic Resource Center
1-800-423-0563

For permission to use material from this text, contact us by:
Phone: 1-800-730-2214
Fax: 1-800-730-2215
Web: http://www.thomsonrights.com

Wadsworth/Thomson Learning
10 Davis Drive
Belmont, CA 94002-3098
USA

Asia
Thomson Learning
60 Albert Street, #15-01
Albert Complex
Singapore 189969

Australia
Nelson Thomson Learning
102 Dodds Street
South Melbourne, Victoria 3205
Australia

Canada
Nelson Thomson Learning
1120 Birchmount Road
Toronto, Ontario M1K 5G4
Canada

Europe/Middle East/Africa
Thomson Learning
Berkshire House
168-173 High Holborn
London WC1V 7AA
United Kingdom

Latin America
Thomson Learning
Seneca, 53
Colonia Polanco
11560 Mexico D.F.
Mexico

Spain
Paraninfo Thomson Learning
Calle/Magallanes, 25
28015 Madrid, Spain

**Library of Congress
Cataloging-in-Publication Data**

Smith, Donald E.P.
  Critical thinking: building the basics/
Donald E. P. Smith, Glenn M. Knudsvig, Timothy L. Walter.—2nd ed.
    p. cm.—(Study skills/critical thinking)
  Includes bibliographical references.
  ISBN 0-534-59976-1
  1. Critical thinking.   2. Critical thinking—Problems, exercises, etc.
I. Knudsvig, Glenn M.   II. Walter, Tim.   III. Title.   IV. Series.

BF441 .S625 2002
160—dc21   2002016786

CONTENTS

PART III:
Learning from Your Computer

PREFACE

Critical Thinking: Building the Basics is an easy-to-use, interesting book that will help you improve your basic critical thinking strategies. It is designed to be used across the curriculum in any course. Whether you are a student in a beginning English course or a freshman seminar, a graduate student in a psychology course, a medical school student, or an independent learner, you will find this book appropriate and user friendly.

How can any one book be appropriate for all students across the curriculum? We carefully assessed the basic critical thinking strategies that good students use and designed the book to teach these strategies. We tested the book on more than 2,000 students at every level, from freshmen through graduate school. When we asked students what they could do better after using the book, they described several important outcomes. They now had strategies for focusing on information and organizing it and processing it in a new way that helped them think about and remember information better. In addition, the new strategies helped them make sense out of information that previously had been complex and difficult to understand.

Students who have learned efficient and effective basic critical thinking strategies are likely to learn higher level critical thinking strategies with relatively ease. Without the basic critical thinking strategies, students at all levels struggle, unnecessarily. After students spend a few hours working through *Critical Thinking: Building the Basics*, they gain basic critical thinking strategies that enhance their ability to focus, organize, categorize, process, and retrieve information. They think and learn information in more logical ways, which improves their ability to move up to higher levels of thinking.

This book is easy to use; it is lean and to the point. We have found that we can teach critical thinking strategies very rapidly as long as students follow the instructions carefully and complete each exercise. After completing the exercises, they can check their learning by using the answer key to confirm that they are indeed learning the strategies.

Part I covers critical thinking strategies. Part II asks students to apply the strategies to their own work. We know that unless students can immediately apply them, they are less likely to adopt the strategies as a lifelong means of thinking critically about everything they see and hear. It is for this reason that we have emphasized the across-the-curriculum approach to teaching basic critical thinking. When students see how easy it is to learn and apply the strategies to the courses in which they are enrolled, everyone benefits. This approach is far superior to teaching the strategies in isolation. Part III shows students how to apply the critical thinking strategies to information presented to them on a computer.

We want to acknowledge the more than 2,000 students who worked through the various versions of this book to help us arrive at the most efficient and effective book possible. Many faculty and staff at public and private colleges and universities around the country have used the book with traditional and nontraditional learners. Whether at community colleges, small private institutions, or large state universities, the faculty and staff have been wonderful about using and endorsing the book. We wish to thank several people whose reviews of the book have dramatically enhanced the creation of what they have called the "essential primer for critical thinking."

In particular, we would like to thank the following reviewers:

Anatole Anton, San Francisco State University

Robert L. Arend, Miramar College

Karen Beatty Sookram, Doane College

Kevin Galvin, East Los Angeles College

Randall E. Osborne, Indiana University East

Katherine Ploeger, CSU Stanislaus

Introduction

Some of you bought this book because the title and the description attracted your attention; it looks as if the book will help you become a stronger thinker. Others bought the book because it was assigned for a course you are taking; in this case, the instructor wants to ensure that you have every opportunity to become a better learner and thinker. Whatever your reason for having the book, it is important for you to know that more than 2,000 students throughout the United States have used earlier versions and can tell you that it accomplishes what we intended: to help students learn basic critical thinking strategies, on which higher level thinking is based, and to make the thinking process more orderly and effective. Once you have learned the basic strategies, more advanced strategies will come much easier.

The students who have tested the strategies have provided valuable feedback on what was useful and what needed to be revised in each subsequent version. Thus, you will be able to benefit from not only our own research as authors and teachers but also the experience of the many students who contributed ideas. The process of tryouts and feedback has enabled us to condense the book to a simple and understandable form. You can work through it on your own at your own pace or as part of a course.

The book is divided into three parts. Part I enables you to learn the basic strategies by applying them to material from a wide variety of subject areas. This part allows you to see how applicable the strategies are to every area of information you might need to deal with. Part II shows you how to apply the strategies to your own work and to the information you want to be able to think about, learn, and remember. Part III shows you how to apply the same learning and thinking strategies that you have used with the printed page to information that you read on a computer screen.

We have provided an answer key for many of the exercises. Learn to use this effectively so that you can get feedback on how well you are learning the strategies. The answer key will give you a sense of comfort because you will know whether you are on track and making satisfactory progress. We—and many of the students who have used these materials—strongly recommend a way to check your own understanding: talk with friends, classmates, family members, and others about what you are learning. The more you share your learning with others, the more enjoyable and profitable it becomes for you.

PART I

A Basic Strategy for Learning and Thinking Smart

Do you consider yourself to be a really good thinker? a really good learner? And what about your instructors or your employers: do they consider you to be a good thinker? a good learner?

If you didn't answer with a loud *yes* to these questions, join the group. Most students often feel dissatisfied with the:

- **quality** of their work, of their output. They remember too many examples of

  —not showing that they can think clearly,

  —not giving good answers on essay tests,

  —not asking smart or useful questions in class,

  —not understanding something they have read,

  —not remembering what they heard in class.

- the **time** and **effort** it takes them to understand something, or to think clearly about a topic.

One of the problems is that much of what you are expected to do requires what are sometimes called *higher order* thinking skills (for example, analyzing, comparing, reflecting). But if you are like a lot of people you haven't had the opportunity to learn or to refine some of the basic "lower" and "mid-level" thinking skills on which the higher levels build. Many of you haven't yet developed any sure-fire strategies to help you acquire the basic information needed to operate at the higher levels.

A dominant characteristic of people who think smart and learn smart is that they seem to know what questions to ask at every stage when they are trying to learn something or to solve a problem. They know what information they need at each step as they work toward a goal—whether the goal is to relate lecture notes to a reading assignment, to contribute to a class discussion on a novel, to write a short paper, or to study for an exam.

In this book you will learn a strategy built around a series of questions that will help you:

- learn in a more efficient way,

- think more clearly and critically,

- proceed to more complex questions and topics,

- solve problems with more skill.

A Typical Student Situation

One of the most common situations facing you as you study, read, write, converse, or take exams is that you need to be able to understand, define, and describe the following:

- topics and subject matter that are fairly objective and straight-forward (we didn't say *easy*, just *objective*)—for example, *the function of veins in blood circulation, steps in making a chemical compound, the parts of speech in a foreign language.*

- topics and subject matter that are less objective, less concrete, less obvious—for example, ideas and concepts such as *capitalism, global warming, welfare reform, genetic mutation, strategies for computer programming, fractal geometry, principles of physics.*

You may need to know these topics only "in isolation," that is, without having to relate them to other subject matter; or you may need to know them so well that you can relate them to other topics and deal with them on a higher level. Whatever the need, many students become discouraged because they can't seem to understand some topics clearly. They have not learned or been trained to think in a clear and focused way.

The strategy introduced in this book will help remedy this problem. It will help you obtain the critical information you need for starting to think about and work with a topic. It is built on asking, and trying to answer, several basic questions. This approach will work for you because (1) good questions help you identify the information you need and (2) the quality or completeness of your answer or information will give you feedback as to whether you are on the right track.

THE TCDR STRATEGY:
TOPIC—CLASS—DESCRIPTION—RELEVANCE

To get you started right away, here is the strategy. Use it when you need to get a clear basic understanding of a topic, an understanding that will enable you to think about the topic in a critical and intelligent way. Always make sure that you ask and try to answer these **key questions** about what you are learning or investigating so that you will be able to relate or apply it to other material.

1. **What is the TOPIC I must understand?** (**T**CDR)

   What are the key topics

   —of the textbook chapter as a whole?

   —of the page I am reading now?

   —of the lecture as a whole?

   —of the lecture at this very minute?

   —of the board issue we are discussing?

   —of the part I need to deal with right now?

2. **What is the overall CLASS to which this topic belongs?** (**T**C**DR**)

   —What is the whole of which this topic is a part?

   —What is the "main heading" under which this topic is being presented?

3. **What is the DESCRIPTION of the topic?** (**TC**D**R**)

   —What are its characteristics? its features? its properties?

   —What does it "look" like?

   —How would you describe it so that someone else would be able to recognize an example of this topic, whether in reading material, hearing about it, or on observing it in real life?

4. What is the RELEVANCE of the topic? (TCD**R**)

—What is its importance—to you, to other people, to some other topic being considered?

—What is it used for?

—What role does it play in understanding or explaining something else?

—How does it affect something else?

Look at this example of a simple piece of information that actually answers all four key questions.

A hammer is a tool, consisting of a handle with a heavy "head" placed on one end, used for pounding.

a hammer	the **topic** of the material
a tool	the **class,** the higher level, the main heading
a handle with a heavy head on one end	the **description,** the characteristics
used for pounding	the **relevance** or use

Practice Item Read the following definition and complete the matching task below:

A chair is a piece of furniture consisting of a horizontal surface supported by three or more legs and used for sitting on.

Match the items in column B to the correct label in column A by drawing a line between them.

A	B
topic	*used for sitting on*
class	*a chair*
description	*consisting of a flat surface, supported by three or more legs*
relevance	*a piece of furniture*

Reminder: Compare your answers with those in the Answer Key (p. 91) on practice items throughout the text.

As you proceed through this book you will receive lots of practice in using topic, class, description, and relevance. The exercises in Part I enable you to apply the TCDR strategy to information from texts chosen by the authors of this book; the exercises in Part II ask you to apply the TCDR strategy to information found in your own course texts or other reading assignments.

GOOD ANSWERS TO KEY QUESTIONS

As a student, the general question you will ask—and be asked—most often is the familiar *"what is x?"*, as in *"what is evaporation?"* or *"what is capitalism?"* Sometimes it is expressed as *"define x,"* as in *"define photosynthesis"* or *"define psychotherapy."*

Merely knowing the answers to these questions is seldom an end in itself (except on a test of definitions). Instead, the answers to such questions provide the basis for learning and thinking about related topics or for answering more complex questions. Nevertheless it is absolutely essential that you have good definitions. You need accurate information at this stage or any subsequent thinking or application will not only be difficult but quite likely incorrect.

You will be certain that you know at least the basics about any topic when you are able to give a definition of that topic that includes the answers to the four questions below.

1. **What is the topic I must understand?**
2. **What is the overall class to which this topic belongs?**
3. **What is the description of the topic?**
4. **What is the relevance of the topic?**

Let TCDR work for you.

EXERCISE SET A: Introduction to TCDR

The first set of practice items is designed to allow you to become familiar with the four key questions introduced previously (pages 3 and 4).

Note: The following few items and some others throughout the book may be quite simple. This is intentional. Many students complain that practice exercises in their courses don't always help them learn because they can't understand the content on which the exercise is based. Thus we will always start with simple content and then move to more difficult content. In this way you can focus on the model being learned.

DIRECTIONS

The following three pages include a series of passages and a question based on each one. Three pairs of answers are given for each question. One item of each pair is a **good** answer and tells you what you needed to know; the other is **bad** and gives you incomplete information.

- Circle each answer as **good** or **bad**.

- Tell which of these pieces of information is missing from the bad answer: **topic, class, description, or relevance.**

Fish are animals that have backbones and are able to live in water throughout their entire lives. They breathe with gills rather than with lungs. In place of legs they have fins. Their bodies are covered with hard scales that overlap like roof shingles. They provide humans with one of their most important sources of food.

Question: What are fish?

good / bad

1. a. Fish are animals that live in water and are used for food.

good / bad

b. Fish are animals that live in water and are a source of food. They have a backbone, gills, fins and a covering of scales.

What part is missing from the bad answer?_____

good / bad

2. a. Fish are animals that live in water and have a backbone, gills, fins and a covering of scales. They're used for food.

good / bad

b. Fish are animals that live in water. They have a backbone, gills, fins and a covering of scales.

What part is missing? _____

good / bad

3. a. Fish live in water. They have a backbone, gills, fins and a covering of scales. They're used for food.

good / bad

b. Fish are animals that live in water. They have a backbone, gills, fins and a covering of scales. They're used for food.

What part is missing? _____

Enraged by attacks on their revenue and their dignity, John's supporters marched on London in 1215 c.e. and were welcomed by the townspeople and clergy, who had also suffered from John's demands. The barons demanded that the king accept a charter that would limit his power. John roared angrily, "Why do they not ask for my kingdom?" but he had to yield. The document John signed was the Magna Carta, or Great Charter.

Question: <u>What was the Magna Carta?</u>

good / bad

4. a. The Magna Carta was a document signed by King John that limited the king's power.

good / bad

b. The Magna Carta was a document that limited the king's power.

What part is missing? _____

good / bad

5. a. The Magna Carta was a document signed by King John that limited the king's power.

good / bad

b. The Magna Carta was a document signed by King John.

What part is missing? _____

good / bad

6. a. The Magna Carta was signed by King John and limited the king's power.

good / bad

b. The Magna Carta was a document signed by King John that limited the king's power.

What part is missing? _____

Bromine is a heavy, dark orange liquid used mainly in making ethyl gasoline. Some bromine is used in making dyes and medicines called *bromides*. A large plant that takes bromine from sea water is located in Freeport, Texas. The world produces about 100 times as much bromine now as it did before the sea water process was designed.

Question: <u>What is bromine?</u>

good / bad

7. a. Bromine is a liquid used in making gasoline and medicines.

good / bad

b. Bromine is a liquid, heavy and dark orange, used in making gasoline and medicine.

What part is missing? _____

good / bad

8. a. Bromine is a liquid that is heavy and dark orange.

good / bad

b. Bromine is a liquid, heavy and dark orange, used in making gasoline and medicine.

What part is missing? _____

good / bad

9. a. Bromine is a liquid, heavy and dark orange, used in making gasoline and medicine.

good / bad

b. Bromine is heavy and dark orange. It's used in making gasoline and medicine.

What part is missing? _____

DIRECTIONS

Read the passages and answer the questions for each one.

10. There are more than 30,000 different kinds of fish, many of which we use for food. A favorite sea food is salmon. Most salmon live in the sea, but they lay their eggs in freshwater streams. To reach fresh water, salmon swim upstream, battling rushing currents and leaping up swift waterfalls. During these up-stream journeys, called runs, many salmon are caught in nets and traps to be canned for use as food.

What is the:

1. topic? _____

2. class? _____

3. description as provided here? _____

_____

4. relevance as stated here? _____

_____

11. Iodine is a chemical found in sea water and in stalks of kelp, a type of seaweed. The kelp is dried and burned, and iodine is removed from the ashes. In addition, some kinds of seafood, especially shellfish like shrimp and lobster, supply iodine needed in the diet. The "iodine" that is used as an antiseptic is a solution of iodine in alcohol, better known as tincture of iodine. Pure iodine is a silvery-gray flaky material.

Question: What is iodine?

One learner's answer: Iodine, which is contained in sea water, kelp, and shellfish, is silvery-gray and flaky. It is used as an antiseptic.

1. Your evaluation of the answer: *good   bad*

2. What part, if any, is missing? _____

3. Now rewrite the answer to make it a good answer. (Note that there is no one best order for the information, except that the class should be with the topic.)

   _____

   _____

   _____

12. An ordinary rain cloud is a form of moisture. It is made up of billions of tiny water droplets. Sometimes two tiny drops will bump together and make one larger drop. When the drops become so heavy that air drafts and winds cannot hold them up, gravity pulls the particles down to earth and rain falls. One result is that plants and animals can continue to live and grow.

Question: What is rain?

One learner's answer: Rain is a form of moisture essential to the life and growth of plants and animals.

1. Your evaluation: *good   bad*

2. What part, if any, is missing? _____

3. Now rewrite the answer to make it a good answer.

   _____

   _____

   _____

   _____

EXERCISE SET B: Identifying Topic and Class

This series of practice items will focus on only **topic** and **class** so that their identification will become second nature to you. If you are to become a clear thinker, writer, and reader, you first must be clear about what the topic is that you are studying or discussing or incorporating into a larger problem or issue. Then you must carefully identify the class of the topic so that you can find the appropriate description as well as information on relevance.

An example: Two people discussing the topic of fishing might have some difficulties in communicating if they do not realize that one thinks of fishing under the category of a business and the other thinks about it only as a form of recreation. Clearly the information related to relevance would be different.

Another example: Both the description and the relevance regarding the topic of capitalism would include different information depending on whether it is being thought of as a political system or an economic system.

Note: The passages used in Exercise Sets B and C will be very short so that you can make faster decisions and get more practice. Later you will practice using extended passages from commonly used textbooks.

DIRECTIONS

One or more words are underlined in each of the following short passages. Based only on the content of the passage, determine if the underlined item answers the question "what is the topic?" or the question "what is the class?" Place a check by the correct choice.

1. <u>Trout</u> are game fish. Although most trout prefer fresh water, they are members of the salmon family.

    _____ topic?

    _____ class?

2. Trout are game fish. Although most trout prefer fresh water, they are members of the <u>salmon</u> family.

    _____ topic?

    _____ class?

3. Trout are game fish. One variety, <u>rainbow trout,</u> originally were found in western streams, but they have been stocked in eastern streams by fish conservationists.

    _____ topic?

    _____ class?

4. "<u>Steelheads</u>" are rainbow trout that are landlocked in lakes or that have gone to sea.

    _____ topic?

    _____ class?

5. "Steelheads" are <u>rainbow trout</u> that are landlocked or that have gone to sea.

    _____ topic?

    _____ class?

6. Although rainbow trout was the topic in number 3, it is the

    _____ in number 5.

Therefore: **a word that is the topic in one instance can be the class in another.** This is one reason why you must be a careful thinker while studying or communicating with others.

7. Order these items from most general to most specific; 1 = most general, and 4 = most specific.

    trout   (   )   salmon   (   )
    steelhead (   )   rainbow trout (   )

Thus, each of the items can be either a topic or a class, depending on the context of what is being said.

8. Goats, like other <u>cattle,</u> have a stomach peculiar to grass eaters that allows them to store food for later chewing.

    _____ topic?

    _____ class?

9. Goats, like other cattle, are of several varieties. <u>Swiss goats</u> have pointed ears. <u>Nubian goats,</u> dark in color, have drooping ears, and are milk producers. The <u>third type,</u> which includes Angoras, is remarkable for its production of wool.

   ____ topic?

   ____ class?

10. <u>Goats,</u> like other cattle, are of several varieties. There are three subclasses of goats. Swiss goats have pointed ears. Nubian goats, dark in color, have drooping ears and are milk producers. The third subclass is remarkable for its production of wool.

   ____ topic?

   ____ class?

EXERCISE SET C: Categorizing Information

DIRECTIONS

In each of the following short excerpts from textbooks, one or more words are underlined. Decide which question the underlined word or words answer in the context of the passage. Place a check next to your choice. The first one is already done.

1. One of the instruments used to study the weather is the <u>barometer.</u>

   ____ What is the relevance, or the use, of the topic?

   <u>X</u> What is the topic?

2. This chemical is <u>used in the manufacture of soap.</u>

   ____ What is the relevance, the use?

   ____ What is the class for the topic?

3. The location of any spot can be determined by using the fine lines <u>that crisscross the map from north to south and from east to west.</u> These lines are . . .

___ What is the topic?

___ What is the description?

4. The inhabitants of this region make a curious kind of music through the use of a wide variety of <u>instruments.</u> First, of course, is the drum which . . .

___ What is the description?

___ What is the class for the topic?

5. <u>Sandstone,</u> on the other hand, is formed from sediment cemented together as a result of pressure.

___ What is the description?

___ What is the topic?

6. The suit is constructed of materials designed <u>to protect people from the burning rays of the sun.</u>

___ What is the relevance?

___ What is the class?

7. With such extremes of temperature and lack of air pressure on the moon, people need such a suit <u>to stay alive.</u>

___ What is the topic?

___ What is its relevance?

8. Although most trout prefer fresh water, they are members of the <u>salmon family.</u>

___ What is the class?

___ What is its description?

9. A parking meter is a <u>device</u> that indicates the time spent by a vehicle in a parking space.

___ What is the topic?

10. <u>Cells</u> were first described by . . .

_____ topic?

_____ class?

11. A phagocyte is a <u>body cell</u> that attacks germs.

_____ relevance?

_____ class?

12. <u>It is resistant to both heat and chemicals,</u> so parts made from it are commonly found in production machines.

_____ description?

_____ relevance?

13. In addition to its other roles, petroleum coke is <u>used in the production of whetstone.</u>

_____ relevance?

_____ description?

14. Recovery of such chemicals from their natural states is <u>important for medical and scientific purposes.</u>

_____ description?

_____ relevance?

15. Such devices may be used to <u>filter out the blue light and thus bring out the white tone of the cloud.</u>

_____ relevance?

_____ topic?

16. The <u>pituitary</u> is one of the glands of the body. It produces a number of hormones which . . .

_____ topic?

_____ description?

17. Uranus is farther from the sun than is earth. If you have keen vision, you can sometimes see the planet <u>Uranus</u> on a clear night.

    ___ topic?

    ___ relevance?

18. The green coloring matter in plants is called *chlorophyll*. It is <u>found both in the leaves of plants and in the stem.</u>

    ___ relevance?

    ___ description?

19. The method by which a government controls economic activities is referred to as <u>regulation.</u>

    ___ class?

    ___ topic?

20. <u>Silicone</u> is the name applied to a large family of compounds.

    ___ description?

    ___ topic?

21. It is for this reason that such materials can be <u>used as containers to hold strong acids.</u>

    ___ description?

    ___ relevance?

22. The heaviest of precious metals is <u>platinum</u>. Only gold and silver are easier to shape.

    ___ topic?

    ___ class?

DIRECTIONS

The following items are designed to give you a chance to review the four categories of information from a different perspective. Choose one of each pair:

1. If you want to find the TOPIC, you could ask:

   _____ What does it look like?

   _____ What is it about?

2. If you want to find the CLASS, you could ask:

   _____ What is it used for?

   _____ What is a general name?

3. If you want to find the DESCRIPTION, you could ask:

   _____ What does it look like?

   _____ What is a good title?

4. If you want to find the RELEVANCE, you could ask:

   _____ What is it about?

   _____ What is it used for?

5. If TOPIC:

   _____ What is it about?

   _____ What is its purpose?

6. If DESCRIPTION:

   _____ What are its characteristics?

   _____ What is a general name?

7. If CLASS:

   _____ Is it possibly a process or a method?

   _____ What does it look like?

8. If RELEVANCE:

   _____ What is this about?

   _____ What is its purpose?

9. If DESCRIPTION:

   ____ What happens first? What next?

   ____ What is it used for?

10. If RELEVANCE:

   ____ Why is it important?

   ____ What does it look like?

DIRECTIONS

These passages name the topic and provide information for one other part of the complete definition. Decide which other part is included and put an x by that item.

1. Look for a piece of fine-grained, gray, or creamy-white rock. If it is rather solid but can be scratched easily with the point of your knife, this rock will probably be limestone.

   ____ description?   ____ relevance?

2. There are several kinds of anemometers. The most common kind has three or four cups attached to short metal bars connected to a shaft. The wind, striking the cup, makes the shaft turn . . .

   ____ description?   ____ relevance?

3. The anemometer is used to measure the speed of the wind.

   ____ description?   ____ relevance?

4. Only about 3% of all salt produced is used on our tables. It is used in brines for refrigerating, in the manufacture of glass and soap, and in making many other chemicals.

   ____ description?   ____ relevance?

5. Slate, the material of which some roofs and school blackboards are made, is a metamorphic rock.

   ____ description?   ____ relevance?

EXERCISE SET D: TCDR in Textbooks

One of the most difficult of the four questions is often "what is the relevance or use of the topic?" It is easy to answer this question when you read or hear such things as:

X was developed in order to explain . . .

Y ensures that the data is reported correctly.

Z was designed to be used in preventing . . .

But often, especially when the topic is a concept, idea, subjective term, or the like, the relevance or use is not overtly stated. Instead it is implied by the context in which it occurs. In these instances, your role is to think about why the concept or idea has been introduced. What is its intended purpose or use in this context? How does it contribute to the discussion?

Needless to say, it does not do you much good as a learner and thinker to know only the description of a topic but not how it relates to or helps explain other topics. Thus you must try to determine the relevance. This in itself is a higher level thinking skill because it may sometimes require a good deal of analysis, synthesis, hypothesizing, inferencing, and relating.

In some of the practice exercises that follow you will have to read the passages carefully and think about what is the relevance or use of each topic.

DIRECTIONS

A.   Read the textbook excerpt on pages 21 and 22 and answer the questions below based on what you read. Write your answers in the space provided. The passage is from a social science textbook.

This exercise also provides an example of the point made earlier in the book: any item can be the topic at one point in the discussion and later be the name of the class for other items, which might also be considered "subtopics."

B.   Indicate for each answer whether

- you found the answer clearly stated in the text, or

- you "had to think it up," or

- you are not sure how to answer it.

IN TEXT   THINK IT UP   NOT SURE

1. What is the topic? *social science*

   What is the class?   ____   ____   ____

   What is the description? (Write answer below.)

                                         ____   ____   ____

   What is the relevance? (Write answer below.)

                                         ____   ____   ____

2. What is the topic? *anthropology*   ____   ____   ____

   What is the class?   ____   ____   ____

   What is the description?   ____   ____   ____

   What is the relevance?   ____   ____   ____

3. What is the topic? *cultural anthropology*

                                         ____   ____   ____

   What is the class?   ____   ____   ____

   What is the description?   ____   ____   ____

	IN TEXT	THINK IT UP	NOT SURE
What is the relevance?	_____	_____	_____

4. What is the topic? _sociology_

	IN TEXT	THINK IT UP	NOT SURE
What is the class?	_____	_____	_____
What is the description?	_____	_____	_____
What is the relevance?	_____	_____	_____

5. What is the topic? _stratification_

	IN TEXT	THINK IT UP	NOT SURE
	_____	_____	_____
What is the class?	_____	_____	_____
What is the description?	_____	_____	_____
What is the relevance?	_____	_____	_____

Power and the Social Sciences

Social science is the study of human behavior. Actually, there are several social sciences, each specializing in a particular aspect of human behavior and each using different concepts, methods, and data in its studies. Anthropology, sociology, economics, psychology, political science, and history have developed into separate "disciplines," but all share an interest in human behavior.

Power is *not* the central concern of the social sciences, yet all the social sciences deal with power in one form or another. Each of the social sciences contributes to an understanding of the forces that modify the conduct of individuals, control their behavior, and shape their lives. Thus, to fully understand power in society, we must approach this topic in an *interdisciplinary* fashion—using ideas, methods, data, and findings from all the social sciences.

Anthropology

Anthropology is the study of people and their ways of life. It is the most comprehensive of the social sciences. Some anthropologists are concerned primarily with people's biological and physical characteristics: this field is called *physical anthropology*. Other anthropologists are interested primarily in the ways of life of both ancient and modern peoples; this field is called *cultural anthropology.*

Culture is all the common patterns and ways of living that characterize society. The anthropologist tries to describe and explain a great many things: child rearing and education; family arrangements; language and communication; technology; ways of making a living; the distribution of work; religious beliefs and values; social life; leadership patterns; and power structures.

Power is part of the culture or the way of life of a people. Power is exercised in all societies, because all societies have systems of rewards and sanctions designed to control the behavior of their members. Perhaps the most enduring structure of power in society is the family: power is exercised within the family when patterns of dominance and submission are established between male and female and parents and children. Societies also develop structures of power outside the family to maintain peace and order among their members; to organize individuals to accomplish large-scale tasks; to defend themselves against attack; and even to wage war and exploit other peoples.

In our study of power and culture, we shall examine how cultural patterns determine power relationships. We shall examine patterns of authority in traditional and modern families and the changing power rule of women in society. We shall examine the origins and development of power relationships, illustrating them with examples of societies in which power is organized by family and kinship group (polar Eskimos), by tribe (Crow Indians), and by the state (the Aztec empire). Finally, as a case study, we shall look at the controversy over "sociobiology"—that is, the extent to which genetics of culture determines behaviors.

Sociology

Sociology is the study of relationships among individuals and groups. Sociologists describe the structure of formal and informal groups, their functions and purposes, and how they change over time. They study social institutions (such as families, schools, churches), social processes (for example, conflict, competition, assimilation, change), and social problems (crime, race relations, poverty, and so forth). Sociologists also study social classes.

All societies have some system of classifying and ranking their members—a system of *stratification*. In modern industrial societies, social status is associated with the various roles that individuals play in the economic system. Individuals are ranked according to how they make their living and the control they exercise over the living of others. Stratification into social classes is determined largely on the basis of occupation and control of economic resources.

Power derives from social status, prestige, and respect, as well as from control of economic resources. Thus, the stratification system involves the unequal distribution of power.

DIRECTIONS

The next three passages are from a chapter in an astronomy textbook.

A. Define the topics <u>comet</u> and <u>comet nucleus</u> by answering the questions listed below. Write your answers in the space provided.

B. Indicate for each answer whether:

- you found the answer clearly stated in the text, or
- you "had to think it up," or
- you are not sure how to answer it.

	IN TEXT	THINK IT UP	NOT SURE
1. What is the topic? <u>*comet*</u>	____	____	____
What is the class?	____	____	____
What is the description?	____	____	____
What is the relevance?	____	____	____

2. What other topics that are equivalent to comets would you expect to find in this chapter?_____

_____

	IN TEXT	THINK IT UP	NOT SURE
3. What is the topic? *comet nucleus*	____	____	____
What is the class?	____	____	____
What is the description?	____	____	____
What is the relevance?	____	____	____

_____

Comets

Comets are the most spectacular of the small bodies in the solar system. When they pass through the inner solar system near the Earth, they can be seen drifting slowly from night to night among the stars. (Writers sometimes incorrectly describe comets as "flashing across the sky" like shooting stars. They do not. They seem to hang motionless and ghostly among the stars. Their motion relative to the stars can be detected by the naked eye only after a few hours.)

Comets have several parts, as seen in Figure 13-2 and 13-3. The brightest part is the comet head. The comet tail is a fainter glow extending out of the head, usually pointing away from the Sun. Although a typical comet tail can be traced for only a few degrees by the naked eye, binoculars or long-exposure photos may reveal fainter extensions of the tail extending tens of degrees or even extending clear across the night sky. A telescope reveals a brilliant, starlike point at the center of the comet head. At the center of this bright point is the comet nucleus, which is the only substantial, solid part of the comet, but is too small to be resolved by telescopes on Earth. Studies reveal that a typical comet nucleus is a worldlet of dirty ice only about 1 to 20 km (a few miles) across—tiny compared to most planets and moons! The gas and dust that make up the rest of the comet's head and tail are material emitted from the nucleus. As the comet nucleus moves through the inner solar system, the sunlight warms it and causes the ice to evaporate into the form of gas. This gas, together with dislodged dust grains from the dirt in the nucleus, is then carried away . . .

DIRECTIONS

A. Define <u>photometry</u> by answering the questions after the following excerpt. This, too, is from the astronomy textbook.
B. In the space that follows the excerpt, write three other questions that the passage answers.

Photometry

Pictures of astronomical objects are interesting, of course, but much astronomical work requires measuring an object's brightness—the amount of light coming from it at all wavelengths or at selected ranges of wavelengths (such as blue to green). This is called photometry. By giving a precise measure of the amount of light at various wavelengths, photometry allows astronomers to measure temperature, composition, and other properties of a remote object. Until a few decades ago, this was done by measuring the size and density of the image on a photograph. Today it is done much more precisely with electronic devices. The basic device is a photomultiplier placed at the telescope's focus. Each photon of light collected by the telescope strikes the photomultiplier surface, which is designed to release a shower of electrons with each photon impact. In some designs, each electron strikes a surface and releases more electrons, thus multiplying the effect into a weak electric current that can be measured. Measurement of the current tells the number of photons arriving from the astronomical object, thus giving a measurement of its light intensity.

In recent years, these techniques have been extended into video-imaging devices that can produce TV images of objects too faint to photograph. Most important of . . .

	IN TEXT	THINK IT UP	NOT SURE
1. What is the topic? *photometry*	____	____	____
What is the class?	____	____	____

	IN TEXT	THINK IT UP	NOT SURE

What is the description?   ____   ____   ____

What is the relevance?   ____   ____   ____

2. What are three additional questions answered by the passage?

DIRECTIONS

A. What is <u>planetology?</u> Define by answering the questions.
B. What is <u>comparative planetology?</u> Define by answering the questions.
C. Write one other question that the passage answers.

_____

Comparative Planetology: An Approach to Studying Planets

Planetology is the study of individual planets and systems of planets. In the early years of planetary studies through telescopes, each planet tended to be characterized as a world unto itself: Certain markings could be glimpsed on Mars; Jupiter had a different type of markings; Saturn had rings; and so on. But in recent decades, as we have come to learn more about planets' surfaces, atmospheres, interiors, and evolution, with spacecraft and with sophisticated astronomical instruments, a new style of planetology has come into being. It is called *comparative planetology:* a systematic study of how planets compare with each other, why they are different, and why certain planets have certain similarities.

In comparative planetology, each planet and moon is regarded as an experiment that teaches us what type of environment evolves if you start with a certain mass, with a certain composition, at a certain distance from the Sun. A good example of this approach comes from . . .

_____

	IN TEXT	THINK IT UP	NOT SURE

1. What is the topic? _planetology_   ____   ____   ____

   What is the class?   ____   ____   ____

   What is the description?   ____   ____   ____

   What is the relevance?   ____   ____   ____

2. What is the topic? _comparative planetology_

                                         ____   ____   ____

   What is the class?   ____   ____   ____

   What is the description?   ____   ____   ____

   What is the relevance?   ____   ____   ____

3. What is one other question answered by the passage?

DIRECTIONS

A. Answer the two questions below with information from a chemistry textbook. (Write your answers in the space following the excerpt.) Remember that each of your answers is actually the answer to the four key subquestions. The two questions are:

"What is <u>filtration</u>?"

"What is <u>distillation</u>?"

B. Write an evaluation of each of your answers. Do each of your answers to "what is . . . ?" answer the four key questions? If not, why not?

Separation of Mixtures

How would you (1) separate sand from water, (2) separate a mixture of water and ethyl alcohol dissolved in one another, (3) remove sand from table sugar, and (4) remove water from penicillin produced by a mold culture?

One of the chemist's most common problems is separating mixtures into fairly pure substances (Section 1.2) and then purifying these substances further. Some of the more common separation and purification techniques are (1) filtration, (2) distillation, (3) recrystallization, and (4) extraction.

Filtration

To separate sand from water, you could let the water evaporate, although this might take a long time and the water would be lost. You could also pour off the water (decantation), but unless done with great care some of the sand might be poured off with the water.

A physical process that avoids these difficulties is *filtration.* Like many methods for separating mixtures, it is based on the solubility of substances in a liquid solvent (Section 13.2). It can be used to separate (a) two solids if one is highly soluble in a liquid in which the other solid is insoluble or (b) an undissolved solid from a liquid. In this case, sand is insoluble in water and can thus be separated by filtration (see Figure 13.6). The mixture of sand and water is poured into a funnel fitted with a piece of filter paper. Sand, the insoluble component, stays on the filter paper, while the water passes through. The liquid that passes through the filter is called the *filtrate.*

Distillation

Sand can also be separated from water by boiling the water and then condensing and collecting the water vapor in a separate container. This process is called *distillation.* A simple distillation apparatus is shown in Figure 13.7. Such an apparatus is especially useful in separating mixtures of some miscible liquids that are soluble in each other in all proportions, such as water and ethyl alcohol, that have different boiling points. During the distillation process the ethyl alcohol, which has the lower boiling point, vaporizes more readily than the water. Thus, the liquid formed by condensing the vapor contains more ethyl alcohol than water. If this condensed distillate is redistilled, its vapor will be even richer in ethyl alcohol and the liquid remaining in the distillation flask will be richer in water. If this distillation and redistillation process is repeated often enough, the condensed liquid becomes almost pure ethyl alcohol and the higher-boiling-point liquid left in the flask becomes almost pure water.

Your answer to "What is <u>filtration</u>?"

Answer to "What is <u>distillation</u>?"

Evaluation of answers: (Have you answered the four key questions in each of your answers? If not, why not?)

DIRECTIONS

A. Write an answer to each of the questions below on the basis of the information in the passage from an introductory psychology textbook. Write your answers and evaluations in the space following the excerpt. The questions are:

1. "What is <u>psychoanalysis</u>?" (or "Define psychoanalysis.")
2. "What is <u>catharsis</u>?" (or "Define catharsis.")
3. "What is <u>free association</u>?" (or "Define free association.")

B. Write an evaluation of each of your answers. Do they answer the four basic questions? If not, what proved to be difficult?

Psychoanalysis

Psychoanalysis, Sigmund Freud's method of psychotherapy, was the first of the "talk" therapies. Psychoanalysts try to help clients achieve insight into why they do what they do and think what they think (Figure 15.J). Psychoanalysis is therefore described as an "insight-oriented therapy" in contrast to therapies that focus on changing thoughts and behaviors.

Freud believed that psychological problems were the result of unconscious thought processes and that the only way to control self-defending behaviors was to make those processes conscious. Bringing them to consciousness, he thought, would release pent-up emotion in a process called *catharsis.*

At first, Freud sought to gain access to his clients' unconscious through hypnosis. He abandoned that approach, however, after he discovered that many clients immediately forgot the insights they had gained while under hypnosis. He developed other methods of bringing unconscious material to consciousness: free association, dream analysis, and transference.

Free Association

Free association is a method that Freud and his patients developed together. (Actually, a more accurate translation of the German expression would be "free intrusion.") In free association, the client lies on a couch, starts thinking about a particular symptom or problem, and then reports everything that comes to mind—a word, a phrase, a visual image. The client is instructed not to omit anything, not to censor anything that might be embarrassing, and not to worry about trying to express everything in complete sentences.

The therapist listens for links and themes that might tie the patient's fragmentary remarks together.

Your answer to "What is <u>psychoanalysis</u>?"

Your answer to "What is <u>catharsis</u>?"

Your answer to "What is <u>free association</u>?"

Evaluation of your answers: (Have you answered the four key questions in each of your answers? If not, why not?)

Question 1

Question 2

Question 3

DIRECTIONS

A. Read the following excerpt from a social science textbook and in the space following the excerpt write an answer to the question: "What is <u>fascism</u>?"

B. Write an evaluation of your answer. Does it answer the four basic questions? If not, why not?

Fascism: The Supremacy of Race and Nation

Fascism is an ideology that asserts the *supremacy of the nation or race over the interests of individuals or groups.* In the words of Benito Mussolini, "Everything for the state; nothing against the state; nothing outside of the state." The state is the embodiment of a unifying, ethical "ideal" that stands above the materialistic class interest of a marxist or the selfish individualism of the liberals.

Fascism perceives the state as not merely a governmental bureaucracy but *the organic life* of a whole people. According to Mussolini, "The Italian nation is an organism having ends, life, and means of action superior to those of the separate individuals or groups of individuals which compose it."

Answer to "What is <u>fascism</u>?"

Evaluation of your answer: (Have you answered the four key questions in each of your answers? If not, why not?)

DIRECTIONS

A. Underline in the following passage (from a psychology textbook) the information that seems to you to answer the question: "How are <u>primary groups</u> described?" (That is, find answers to "What is the description of <u>primary groups</u>?" or "What are the characteristics of <u>primary groups</u>?")

B. Then draw a wavy line under the information that seems to you to answer the question: "What is the relevance (impact/importance) of this topic?"

Primary and Secondary Groups

Not all groups are of equal importance to their members. For example, we will more willingly withdraw from a group made up of persons working in our office than from one made up of family or intimate friends. The notions of primary and secondary groups capture this distinction.

Primary groups are characterized by great intimacy among the members. People in these groups do not merely know one another and interact frequently but know one another well and have strong emotional ties. As a result, people gain much of their self-esteem and sense of identity from primary groups.

Moreover, sociologists regard the relationships among primary group members as the essential glue holding social life together. When Morselli (1882) and Durkheim (1897) blamed high suicide rates on modernization, they were claiming that, compared with traditional rural life, more modern societies have negative impacts on primary groups. These early sociologists also believed that people who lack primary group ties cannot obtain the social support needed to sustain them against trouble and despair. By now there is an immense amount of evidence that early sociologists were right about the dire consequences of social isolation. Indeed, sociologists have demonstrated recently that membership in a primary group even greatly reduces many "natural" causes of death (Litwak and Messeri, 1989). However, later in this chapter we shall see that Morselli, Durkheim, and other early sociologists were wrong to assume that modernization substantially increases social isolation: Even in the midst of large, seemingly impersonal cities, primary groups still thrive.

The family is the most common primary group, but many other groups can also become so. Indeed, Charles H. Cooley, who coined the term *primary group,* said a group is primary if its members refer to themselves as "we." Primary groups involve "the sort of sympathy and mutual identification for which 'we' is the national expression" (Cooley, 1909).

Secondary groups consist of less intimate social networks within which people pursue various collective goals but without a powerful sense of belonging. Business organizations, political parties, even model railroad clubs are typically secondary groups. People find it relatively easy to switch from one secondary group to another and refer to themselves and group members as "we" only casually. However, as we shall see in Chapter 20, primary groups often form *within* secondary groups—a process that can produce internal strains. For example, a group of close friends within a business may promote one another to the disadvantage of other employees and perhaps cause the company to operate less efficiently.

Groups, then, are the primary subject matter of sociology. The aim of sociologists is to construct a science of groups, of human social relations. However, not everyone believes that a science of social relations is possible.

DIRECTIONS

A. Underline in the following passage (from a psychology textbook) the information that seems to you to answer the question: "How is the similarity principle described?" (That is, find answers to "What is the description of this topic?") This is a topic in the section on Affiliation.

B. Then draw a wavy line under the information that seems to you to answer the question: "What is the relevance (impact/importance) of this topic?"

Affiliation

Affiliation is the motivation to be with others. Most of us like to be with other people, though not with just anyone. Suppose you are looking for someone to go to the movies with you or to be your lab partner in chemistry. How do you decide whom to ask? Four important influences on your decision are similarity, proximity, mere exposure, and physical attractiveness.

The Similarity Principle

If you could travel back in time and become close friends with any famous historical figure you chose, whom would you choose? Benjamin Franklin, Martin Luther King, Jr., Marie Curie, Agatha Christie, Confucius, Chief Sitting Bull, Susan B. Anthony, Joan of Arc, Sigmund Freud? Those are just suggestions; choose anyone you wish. How would you decide? Many historical figures would probably be interesting to meet, but in choosing a *friend,* you would probably look for someone similar to you or someone you would like to resemble.

How about your close friends? Do they resemble you in ethnic background, political and religious beliefs, academic interests, and attitudes toward sex and drugs? Most people choose friends who resemble themselves in many ways. This tendency is known as the similarity principle.

In one study, researchers at the University of Michigan surveyed 1,000 men living in or around Detroit. They asked the men to list their three closest friends and to provide information about themselves and about their friends, including age, occupation, religious affiliation, and political leanings. It turned out that the friends resembled the men on every variable that was measured in the study (Laumann, 1969).

Moreover, most people choose romantic partners who resemble them in various ways. Both dating couples and married couples tend to resemble each other in age, physical appearance, social class, ethnic identity, religion, intelligence, attitudes and values, and use or abstention from alcohol and tobacco (Burgess & Wallin, 1943: Buss, 1985; Osborne et al., 1978). Well-matched couples are more likely to stay together than couples who are not well matched (Hill, Rubin, & Peplau, 1976).

In a number of experiments to determine what role similar attitudes play in the attraction between people, pairs of subjects have filled out attitude questionnaires and then been shown what was said to be the other's responses. Actually, the experimenter falsified the responses in order to suggest a greater or lesser degree of similarity between the two. Then each subject has been asked how much he or she likes the other person. The results have consistently shown that subjects like partners whose attitudes resemble their own (Byrne, 1971).

DIRECTIONS

A. Underline in the passage below (from a psychology textbook) the information that seems to you to answer the question: "How is group therapy described?" (That is, find answers to "What is the description of this topic?" or "What are the characteristics of this topic?")

B. Then draw a wavy line under the information that seems to you to answer the question: "What is the relevance (impact/importance) of this topic?"

Treating People in Groups

Freud and the other early pioneers of psychotherapy dealt with their clients on a one-on-one basis. Individual psychotherapy has its advantages, most of all privacy. But for many purposes it is helpful to treat clients in groups.

Group Therapy

Group therapy is therapy that is administered to a group of people all at one time. It first came into vogue for economic reasons. Most psychotherapists charge substantial fees for the usual 50-minute session. (They have to charge more per patient than most medical practitioners simply because they see only one patient per hour.) Because middle-class and poor people in need of psychotherapy cannot afford those fees, some therapists began to treat small groups of people, spreading the cost among them.

Group therapy has other advantages as well. Therapists typically try to set up a group of about seven or eight people who are about the same age with similar problems—people who have as much in common with one another as possible. They take comfort when they discover that others share their problems. They learn from each other and are encouraged by each other's successes.

Group therapy sessions give people an opportunity to explore how they relate to others. Clients become aware of how they irritate others and how they can be useful to others. They use group therapy to develop and practice social skills (Bloch, 1986).

DIRECTIONS

A. This item focuses on description and relevance. Underline in the passage below (again from a psychology textbook) the information that seems to you to answer the question: "How is panic disorder described?" (That is, find answers to "What is the description of panic disorder?" or "What are the characteristics of panic disorder?")

The beginning of the section on Anxiety Disorders is included to provide a context.

B. Then draw a wavy line under the information that seems to you to answer the question: "What is the relevance (impact/importance) of this topic?"

Anxiety Disorders

Many psychological disorders are marked by a combination of fear, anxiety, and attempts to avoid anxiety. Anxiety, unlike fear, is generally not associated with a specific situation. We feel fear in the presence of a hungry tiger, but our fear passes as soon as we get away. But we cannot escape the anxiety we experience about dying or about our personal inadequacies. Some degree of anxiety is normal; it becomes a problem only when it interferes with our ability to cope with everyday life.

Panic Disorder

Panic disorder is an emotional disturbance found in about 1% of all American adults and among very few children (Myers et al., 1984; Robins et al., 1984). People with this disorder experience a fairly constant state of moderate anxiety, along with occasional panic attacks, accompanied by chest pains, difficulty in breathing, increased heart rate, sweating, faintness, and shaking (see Figure 14.4). A panic attack generally lasts only a few minutes, although it may last an hour or more. During an attack, most people worry about fainting, dying, or going crazy (Argyle, 1988). After a few such attacks, those worries may grow more intense and may even trigger further attacks.

Panic disorder can become self-perpetuating (Figure 14.5). Many people deal with anxiety by taking a deep breath or two, to help calm themselves down. On the theory that "if a little is good, a whole lot will be better," they may continue breathing deeply, or hyperventilating. Hyperventilation expels carbon dioxide and therefore lowers the carbon dioxide level in the blood. Then if something happens that increases the carbon dioxide level, such as sudden physical activity or an experience that excites the sympathetic nervous system, the carbon dioxide level in the blood increases by a large percentage and stimulates an increased heart rate, trembling, and other symptoms of a panic attack—the very thing the person was trying to avoid (Gorman et al., 1986; Woods et al., 1986). After a few such episodes, the likelihood of further attacks increases. One treatment for panic attacks is to teach the person to avoid hyperventilating (Wolpe & Rowan, 1988).

When people discover that physical exertion sometimes triggers a panic attack, they may decide to avoid any sort of physical activity. As a result, they grow even more sensitive to the effects of physical activity; even slight exertion will raise the level of carbon dioxide in their blood. Consequently, some authorities recommend regular exercise as a treatment for panic attacks (Ledwidge, 1980).

DIRECTIONS

A. Underline in the following passage (from a social science textbook) the information that seems to you to answer the question: "How is conservatism described?" (That is, find answers to "What is the description of conservatism?" or "What are the characteristics of conservatism?")

B. Then draw a wavy line under the information that seems to you to answer the question: "What is the relevance (impact/importance) of this topic?"

Modern Conservatism: Individualism and Traditional Values

Conservatism and Liberalism

In the United States today *conservatism* is associated with classical liberalism. Conservatives in this country retain the early liberal commitment to individual freedom from governmental controls; maximum personal liberty; reliance on individual initiative and effort for self-development, rather than on governmental programs and projects; a free-enterprise economy with a minimum of governmental intervention; and rewards for initiative, skill, risk, and hard work, in contrast to government-imposed "leveling" of income. These views are consistent with the early classical liberalism of Locke, Jefferson, and the nation's Founding Fathers. The result, of course, is a confusion of ideological labels: conservatives today charge modern liberals with abandoning the principles of individualism, limited government, and free enterprise, and today's conservatives claim to be the true "liberals" in society.

Conservativism and Human Nature

Modern conservativism does indeed incorporate much of classical liberalism, but conservatism also has a distinct ideological tradition of its own. Conservatism is not as optimistic as liberalism about human nature. Traditionally, conservatives realized that human nature includes elements of irrationality, intolerance, extremism, ignorance, prejudice, hatred, and violence. Thus they were more likely to place their faith in *law* and *tradition* than in the popular emotions of mass movement. Without the protection of law and tradition, people and societies are vulnerable to terror and violence. The absence of law does not mean freedom, but rather, exposure to the tyranny of terrorism and violence.

Preference for Evolutionary Change

Conservatism sets forth an *evolutionary* view of social progress. Revolutionary change is far more likely to set back society than to improve it. But over time, people can experiment in small ways with incremental changes; continued from generation to generation, this process of evolutionary change leads to a progressive improvement in the condition of humanity. *No government* possesses the wisdom to resolve all problems, but the cumulative experience of society does produce certain workable arrangements for the amelioration of social ills. Gradual progress is possible, but only if people do not destroy the painfully acquired wisdom of the past in favor of new, untried utopian solutions that jeopardize the well-being of society.

DIRECTIONS

A. This exercise once again provides an opportunity to practice finding and writing answers to the four key questions. The passage is from a social science textbook.

"What is the topic?"

"What is the class?"

"What is the description of the topic?"

"What is the relevance of the topic?"

B. Evaluate the completeness of each answer. That is, to what degree were you able to answer each question?

C. Write three additional questions that the passage answers.

Automatic Stabilizers

Automatic stabilizers are government programs that act automatically to counter the effects of economic cycles. For example, since income taxes increase in proportion to one's earnings, the income tax automatically restricts spending habits in times of prosperity by taking larger bites of income. In times of adversity and low earnings, taxes drop automatically. Welfare programs also act automatically to counter economic cycles: in recessions, more people apply for welfare and unemployment payments, and those payments help to offset declines in income.

Monetary Policy

Since banks are the major source of money and credit, the government can control investment spending by making it easy to borrow money from banks. . . .

"What is the topic?"

"What is the class?"

"What is the description of the topic?"

"What is the relevance of the topic?"

Evaluate the completeness of each answer.

- topic

- class

- description

- relevance

Write three additional questions that the passage answers.

This is the final exercise for Part I.

DIRECTIONS

Here is one last practice item from a textbook on language learning. The topic of this passage is <u>conferencing.</u> The chapter title is "Writing as Process and Product"; this section deals with "Feedback on Written Work."

A. Circle the word or words that answer the question: "What is the class to which <u>conferencing</u> belongs in this particular passage?"

B. Underline the information that seems to you to answer the question: "How is conferencing described?" (That is, find answers to "What is the description of <u>conferencing</u>?" or "What are the characteristics of <u>conferencing</u>?")

C. Then draw a wavy line under the information that seems to you to answer the question: "What is the relevance (impact/importance) of this topic?"

Feedback on Written Work

One of the most problematic areas in the domain of writing in a target language is that of feedback to the writer—whether it be from teacher, tutor, peer, or self. Let us first consider oral conferences and written comments from the teacher.

Conferencing

Conferencing, the term used to describe one-to-one consultation between teacher and student during the evolution of a composition, has become one of the buzzwords of writing (Graves 1983, Calkins 1986, Harris 1987). The concern for conferencing sessions is based on the position that an interactive session can help to clear up matters that cannot be handled by written feedback alone. There is, in fact, some research evidence that spoken feedback has advantages over written feedback (Rose 1982). Yet a major problem is that teachers need to find the time to conduct such interactive sessions. One large-scale study in Europe, for instance, found that most teachers do not have time for extensive individual conferences (Freedman 1987), but, even when they do take place, the reality of such teacher-student interactions may fall short of what experts would recommend.

PART II

Making the TCDR Strategy Work for You

As you learned in Part I, when you think about information in terms of **topic, class, description,** and **relevance (TCDR)** you will improve your efficiency and effectiveness as a learner and a thinker. Part II is designed to enable you to practice applying the critical thinking strategy of TCDR to material you will read in your own texts or hear in your classes. By doing so you'll see how appropriate the strategy is to thinking about any type of information you encounter in your courses.

You will find that by using this extensively tested strategy, you can produce the clear thoughts and the kinds of answers that will match those of the people you consider to be outstanding learners and students. The TCDR strategy will help you learn to think about topics in the ways your instructors and textbook writers do; you will be pleased to see how similar your questions and answers are to those of people you consider to be experts in the field.

EXERCISE SET A

Developing Questions and Evaluating Answers

DIRECTIONS

In Exercise Set A you can practice using the TCDR strategy on an excerpt of six pages from *Introduction to Psychology* by James Kalat (pages 60–65). Read these six pages and select several topics that you believe are important ones. These are topics that you might be asked to discuss in class or that you might be asked to relate to other topics for a paper or in an exam.

Your list of possible topics:

Good critical thinking requires that you determine which topics are most important or are most relevant to your purpose.

DIRECTIONS

Select from your list of topics one that you would like to focus on. (In this exercise you may select the topic primarily because of its interest to you, since you do not have a specific need at this moment.)

Your choice of topic:

As you saw in Part I, you can gain clearer understanding of important topics by using the TCDR strategy, first identifying the class to which your topic belongs and then gathering the information on description and relevance.

All the information you gather through TCDR helps you develop good answers to questions about the topics. These questions, many of which you may encounter in discussions, writing assignments, and tests, take many forms. Examples of these are:

- What is . . . (topic x) . . . ?
- Define . . . (topic x) . . .
- Compare and contrast . . . (topic x and topic y) . . .
- Identify the important components of . . . (topic x) . . .
- What is the relationship between . . . (topic x and topic y) . . . ?
- Describe several examples of . . . (topic x) . . .
- What is the significance of . . . (topic x) . . . to . . . (topic y) . . . ?

Your ability to answer questions such as these about any topic you encounter can be increased greatly through the use of TCDR. Through this strategy you will obtain information that will demonstrate that you have thought critically and analytically about the topic(s) at hand.

If you review the questions at the end of textbook chapters, you will find that authors typically provide a variety of questions; some are very straightforward while others may be difficult to interpret. Whatever the form of the questions, TCDR will provide you with the basic structure from which to develop your answers.

DIRECTIONS

Write a question about the topic you selected (page 42). Base your question on one of the examples just listed.

Your question:

DIRECTIONS

Now, read the six pages (60–65) to obtain the TCDR information about the topic before you actually write an answer to your question. You will first determine the **class** of your topic.

Write several possible classes to which your topic (your question) could belong and circle the class that seems most appropriate for this passage.

- _____
- _____
- _____

Now that you have selected a class, select from the material:

1. all the important **descriptors of the topic** and
2. all important information regarding the **relevance of the topic.**

Description

- _____
- _____
- _____
- _____
- _____

Relevance

- _____

- _____

- _____

- _____

- _____

Writing your answer

Now that you have determined the descriptors and relevance, it is time to write a practice answer in which you incorporate the necessary descriptors and any statements about the relevance of the topic.

Write your answer in the following space. Remember that you may not have been given all the descriptors of the topic in the pages you read. You may need to supply descriptors you are aware of from other sources of information. The same is true regarding the information about the relevance of the topic. The excerpt may not have addressed relevance as completely as you would have liked. Nevertheless, your answer may include information that you draw from other sources.

The important thing is that your answer should provide all the description of the topic that is needed and as careful a discussion of the relevance of the topic as is possible. If you have any question about this, check back to Part I to see how each answer includes as much discussion of description and relevance as is available and appropriate.

Your topic:

Your question (from page 43):

Your answer:

Your evaluation:

Now it is time for you to evaluate your answer by responding to the following questions (referring back to Part I if you need to):

Does your answer describe the class to which the topic belongs?

_____ yes   _____ no

Does your answer provide a good description of the topic?

_____ yes   _____ no

Does your answer discuss the relevance of your topic?

_____ yes   _____ no

What are other characteristics or special features of your answer that you think demonstrate good thinking and analysis?

- _____

- _____

- _____

Overall, what grade would you award your answer?

A _____   B _____   C _____   Other _____

Why?

_____

_____

Improving Your Thinking by Getting Feedback

Now that you have written your answer, we suggest that you seek another student's assistance to help you evaluate your use of TCDR. Ask another student with whom you feel comfortable in your course to work with you on this exercise.

Evaluation by a Classmate of Your Application of TCDR

Does your answer describe the class to which the topic belongs?

_____ yes   _____ no
Comments:

Does your answer provide a good description of the topic?

_____ yes   _____ no
Comments:

Does your answer discuss the relevance of your topic?

_____ yes   _____ no
Comments:

Would you evaluate the answer as being worthy of an:

A _____   B _____   C _____   Other _____

Why?

_____

_____

More Points for You to Evaluate

1. If the excerpt provided the only information available to you, would there be enough information to answer the question as well as you would like, or would you need to seek information from other sources?

_____ yes   _____ no, I need to look at other sources.

What additional information would you like to have?

2. Did you find that by using the TCDR strategy you were able to more rapidly structure your answer based on description and relevance?

_____ yes   _____ no

Comments:

3. If you hadn't focused on description and relevance as you read the section, how might your answer have differed from the answer you wrote?

Thinking Point

Why do you think we first ask you to read a short section of a chapter and develop one good question and answer? If you start out by focusing on too much information at once you may be overwhelmed. Once you become comfortable with the TCDR process by focusing on small amounts of information you will be ready to tackle an entire chapter.

TCDR as a Cognitive Strategy

Learning to use TCDR is part of learning to develop what cognitive and developmental psychologists call a **cognitive schema.** A cognitive schema is just that: "a scheme," "a method," "a process" by which you can see, organize, and structure information so that you can understand and remember it better.

In Part II, as you continue using TCDR, the schema will become second nature to you. Whether you're reading articles from textbooks, journals, popular magazines like *Scientific American* or *Newsweek,* or any source, using TCDR will become the schema you use to think about things.

Note: One other point may interest you. Learners frequently complain that they have special difficulty analyzing and understanding certain textbooks and articles, or even lectures, even though they already know something about the subject matter. This may happen partly because the material is not well written or designed or is intended for a different audience. Everyone can relate to being assigned to read textbooks or articles that seem to have been written by professors for professors, rather than by professors for students. But making sense out of information that is poorly presented is another important strategy that you can acquire through TCDR.

TCDR: A Key to Strong Thinking

Your goal is to learn critical thinking strategies that will help you read, listen to, understand, and remember any type of information better. The key to your continued success will be to use TCDR whenever you read and listen. By always focusing on the basic questions posed by TCDR, you'll have a consistent strategy for interpreting, analyzing, organizing, and making sense of the hundreds of pieces of information that you encounter each day of your life.

As you work with and listen to strong critical thinkers, there is one characteristic that stands out: strong thinkers generally believe that an important part of the thinking process includes comparing their ideas with those of their peers. By comparing your answers and ideas with those of your peers and teachers, you will learn to attack problems and questions from different perspectives. You will see that many questions often have no one correct answer.

Strong critical thinkers are people who can take what information is before them and assimilate it into what they already know. They can accommodate information that is new or in conflict with what they know or believe. They develop answers, but are always ready to adjust their answers and perspectives based on new and valid information. This is why the great thinkers and scientists are people who may over a period of time shift their set of beliefs and sometimes take on radically different positions based on new information that contradicts their existing belief system.

Strong critical thinkers are the great creative problem solvers. They are people who are always open to new and different information. They are not tied to one position. They are willing to alter the way in which they see the world based on sound argument and information they collect from many different sources. They are open to assimilating and accommodating new information and to generating new ideas.

This process of thinking and rethinking is part of what education, experience, school and life are all about. You can learn a basic strategy, TCDR, for critical thinking that will dramatically improve your ability to think about information as you see and hear it. But, you must decide that, to be as strong a thinker as possible, you will always reexamine your thoughts and ideas; you will always be ready to listen to new and exciting perspectives and to adjust your positions or beliefs based on the best information available. Only then can you be a truly successful critical thinker.

Developing More Questions

At the beginning of Part II you developed a question and wrote what you believed to be a good answer to the question. Now pretend that you are the instructor of a course in psychology. Take the psychology textbook excerpt (pages 60 – 65) you read and say to yourself, "I am going to develop two more excellent short-answer questions from this section. These will be questions that I think a person reading this section should be able to answer."

DIRECTIONS

Develop two more questions and then use the TCDR strategy to complete answers to the questions. This is not meant to be a complex exercise. We just want you to see how easy it is to think clearly and effectively as you develop questions and answers that assist you in analyzing information.

Your two questions and their answers:

Learning from Another Person's Input

DIRECTIONS

Now that you have two more good questions and answers, share what you have done with a classmate who has gone through the same exercise. See what questions and answers he or she developed from the same material.

Evaluate each of your questions and answers:

1. Does each of your answers name the topic and class?

   ____ yes   ____ no

2. Does each of your answers provide adequate description of the topic?

   ____ yes   ____ no
   Comments:

3. Does each of your answers provide adequate discussion of relevance?

   ____ yes   ____ no
   Comments:

Now that you have had a chance to use TCDR on a section of a textbook we have chosen, the next logical step is to have you choose a textbook from one of your courses and apply TCDR to information from a chapter that you are currently responsible for learning.

EXERCISE SET B

Another Strategy for Improving Thinking

DIRECTIONS

Choose a chapter from one of your textbooks on which you would like to practice using the TCDR strategy.

Write the name of your chapter you're using below:

DIRECTIONS

Check to see if there is a chapter summary at the end of the chapter. If so, please take a few minutes to read the summary. Research on thinking and learning has shown that people who read summaries can more clearly think about and more easily remember information on the important topics in a chapter. Summaries tend to focus on descriptions of important topics and discussions of each topic's relevance.

Did you find a chapter summary and read it?

_____ yes   _____ no

Comments:

If yes, did the summary discuss the most important topics in the chapter, provide a brief description of the topics, and briefly discuss the relevance of the topics?

_____ yes   _____ no

Comments:

DIRECTIONS

Check to see if there is a list of questions at the beginning or the end of the chapter; if there is, read these questions. These are questions the author thinks you should be able to answer if you understand and are able to think about topics within the chapter. These questions, just like the TCDR questions, will help you think critically about information and organize it into meaningful categories.

Did you find a list of questions and read them?

    ____ yes   ____ no

Comments:

DIRECTIONS

Now that you have read the summary and/or the questions and thus have a better understanding of what the chapter will be about, it is time to read the chapter. Go to the beginning of the chapter and choose a section of several pages that you will read.

What pages are you going to read? Pages _____ to _____.

Now read those pages.

From the pages you have read, select several important topics you would like to know more about.

Your list of possible topics:

Now select one of the topics you would like to focus on because of its importance to this section.

Your topic:

DIRECTIONS

Now write a question about the topic you selected that you think is important to answer.

Your question:

Now, from the pages you have chosen, gather the important information about the topic before you write an answer to the question. Please write this information in the space that follows:

CLASS

DIRECTIONS

Write in the possible classes to which the topic could belong and circle the class that seems most appropriate to the question you have asked:

1. _____

2. _____

3. _____

DIRECTIONS

Now that you have selected a class, select from the material (1) all the descriptors of the topic and (2) all important information regarding the relevance of the topic:

Description

1. _____

2. _____

3. _____

4. _____

5. _____

Relevance

1. _____

2. _____

3. _____

4. _____

5. _____

DIRECTIONS

Now that you have determined the descriptors and relevance it is time to write a practice answer in which you incorporate the necessary descriptors and any statements about the relevance of the topic. Write your answers in the following space. Remember that you may not have been given all the descriptors of the topic in the pages you read. You may need to supply descriptors you are aware of from other sources of information.

The same is true of relevance of the topic. The pages may not have addressed relevance as fully as you would like, and you may decide to include information that you draw from other sources.

TOPIC

Your question (from page 52):

Your answer:

Evaluating Your Own Answers

Now it is time for you to evaluate your answer by answering the following questions:

Does your answer describe the class to which the topic belongs?

____ yes   ____ no

Comments:

Does your answer provide a good description of the topic?

____ yes   ____ no

Comments:

Does your answer discuss the relevance of your topic?

____ yes ____ no

Comments:

What are other characteristics of your answer that you think demonstrate good thinking and analysis?

1. _____

2. _____

3. _____

Overall, what grade would you award your answer?

A ____   B ____   C ____   Other ____

Why?

Getting a Second Opinion

Now that you have written your answer, we suggest that you seek another student's assistance to help you evaluate your application of TCDR. Ask another student with whom you feel comfortable in your course.

Your classmate's evaluation of your application of TCDR

Does the answer describe the class to which the topic belongs?

____ yes ____ no

Comments:

Does the answer provide a good description of the topic?

____ yes ____ no

Comments:

Does the answer discuss the relevance of your topic?

_____ yes   _____ no
Comments:

Would you evaluate the answer as being worthy of an:

A _____   B _____   C _____   Other _____
Why?

More Points for You to Evaluate

1. If the four pages you read were the only information available to you, would there be enough information in them to answer the question as well as you would like or would you need to seek information from other sources?

   _____ yes   _____ no, I need to look at other sources.
   What additional information would you like to have?

2. Did you find that by using the TCDR strategy you were able to more rapidly structure your answer based on description and relevance?

   _____ yes   _____ no
   Comments:

3. If you hadn't focused on description and relevance as you read the section, how might your answer have differed from the answer you wrote?

Developing More Questions and Answers

You have just developed a question and written what you believe to be a good answer. Pretend that you are the instructor of your course or the author of the book. Take the chapter from which you developed the question and answer and say to yourself, "I am going to develop five more excellent short-answer essay questions from this chapter."

DIRECTIONS

Using the TCDR strategy, develop five more excellent questions and then write answers to the questions. Write your questions and answers in the notebook you use for the course for which the textbook is assigned. As has been said, in developing your answers you may find that you have to go to other sources such as your course notes, other books, or your friends to find all the information you'll need to answer the questions correctly.

This is not meant to be a complex exercise. It is just meant to help you become comfortable thinking critically about an entire chapter. If you can use the TCDR strategy to analyze an entire chapter and develop five additional good questions and answers you will be well on your way to establishing excellent critical thinking skills.

Your Five Questions and Answers

-
-
-
-
-

An optional exercise

Now that you have five new questions and answers, it once again would be to your advantage to have a friend who is taking the same course review your questions and answers while you review his or her questions and answers. By sharing your critical analyses of what you think good questions and answers look like with your friends, you sharpen your critical thinking skills.

The dialogue between you and friends is part of being a critical thinker. Looking at one another's product, in this case questions and answers, will help you think critically not only about your own performance but about that of your peers. We learn to think critically by openly and honestly sharing our ideas and work. In this case, both of you have produced questions and answers. You now want to share your analysis of what you had to do to arrive at your answers.

As you discuss your questions and answers, you may wish to use the following questions:

1. Would I have answers as complete as the ones I just developed if I hadn't used the TCDR strategy?

2. What does having a "cognitive schema" of TCDR help me do as I read and listen to information?

3. What critical thinking skills would I *not* be using if I didn't approach reading and listening from a TCDR perspective?

4. Why is it easier for people to learn when they develop a TCDR "cognitive schema?"

5. How can I make myself comfortable with automatically using the TCDR strategy as I read and listen? Is there a specific procedure I can follow?

It's Time to Move On

You have done a lot of work in this book. It is no small task to work through all the exercises. But we have found that when students reach this point they are beginning to feel comfortable applying the TCDR critical thinking strategy to their daily course work. It is now time for you to move from this text to a daily routine of reading your course-related materials and listening to lectures and discussions using the TCDR strategy. You can always measure whether you are using the critical thinking strategy by asking several important questions:

- "What are the important topics of discussion?"

- "To what larger body of information or knowledge does this topic belong?"

- "How would I describe these topics?"

- "What is the relevance of these topics?"

- "What important questions can I answer about this information?"

If these questions become part of your daily way of looking at and listening to your world, you will have mastered some of the basic steps of critical thinking. There is much more to the complex patterns of critical thinking than what we have described. But without being able to do what you have learned in these few pages, the more complex processes may well be difficult, if not impossible, to master. Congratulations on what you have accomplished so far. We hope TCDR makes your life, learning, and thinking more predictable, enjoyable, profitable, and exciting.

Reading Excerpt from *Introduction to Psychology* by James Kalat

How Thought Processes and Knowledge Grow: Some Piagetian Terminology

According to Piaget, a child's intellectual development is not merely an accumulation of experience or a maturational unfolding. Rather, the child constructs *new* mental processes as he or she interacts with the environment.

In Piaget's terminology, behavior is based on schemata. A **schema** is an organized way of interacting with objects in the world. For instance, infants have a grasping schema and a sucking schema. Older infants gradually add new schemata to their repertoire and adapt their old ones. This adaptation takes place through the processes of assimilation and accommodation.

In **assimilation** a person applies an old schema to new objects—for example, an infant may suck an unfamiliar object or use the grasp response in trying to manipulate it. In **accommodation** a person modifies an old schema to fit a new object—for example, an infant may suck a breast, a bottle, and a pacifier in different ways or may modify the grasp response to accommodate the size or shape of a new toy.

Infants shift back and forth from assimilation to accommodation. For example, an infant who tries to suck on a rubber ball (assimilating it to her sucking schema) may find that she cannot fit it into her mouth. First she may try to accommodate her sucking schema to fit the ball, if that fails, she may try to shake the ball. She is assimilating her grasping schema to the new object—expanding her motor repertoire to include it—but at the same time she is accommodating that schema—changing it—to fit the ball.

Adults do much the same thing. You are given a new mathematical problem to solve. You try several of the methods you have already learned until you hit on the one schema that works. In other words, you assimilate your old schema to the new problem. If, however, the new problem is quite different from any problem you have ever solved before, you modify (accommodate) your schema until you work out a solution. Through processes like these, said Piaget, intellectual growth occurs.

Piaget's Stages of Intellectual Development

Piaget contended that children progress through four major stages of intellectual development.

1. The sensorimotor stage (from birth to about 1½ years)

2. The preoperational stage (from about 1½ to 7 years)

3. The concrete operations stage (from about 7 to 11 years)

4. The formal operations stage (from about 11 years onward)

The ages given here are approximate. Many people do not reach the stage of formal operations until well beyond age 11, if they reach it at all. Piaget recognized that some children develop at a faster rate than others, but he insisted that all children go through these four stages *in the same order.* Exactly how distinct the stages are is not clear (Keil, 1981).

The Sensorimotor Stage: Infancy

Piaget called the first stage of intellectual development the **sensorimotor stage** because at this early age (birth to 1½ years) behavior consists mostly of simple motor responses to sensory stimuli—for example, the grasp reflex and the sucking reflex. Infants respond to what is present, rather than to what is remembered or imagined. Piaget concluded that infants in the sensorimotor stage are incapable of representational thought—that is, they do not think about objects they cannot see, hear, feel, or otherwise sense. Moreover, Piaget concluded that infants lack the concept of **object permanence.** They do not understand that an object continues to exist when they can no longer see it. (Not only is it "out of sight, out of mind," but "out of sight, out of existence" as well.)

How, you might ask, can we possibly know what a baby does or does not think? We cannot—at least not for sure. Piaget was drawing inferences from the behavior he observed, though other people have drawn different inferences. After we review Piaget's observations, you can draw your own conclusions. (Better yet, study a baby to make your own observations.)

1. *Observation:* From age 3 months to age 6 to 9 months, an infant will reach out to grab a toy only if it is visible. If the toy is partially visible, the infant will reach for it. If it is fully hidden, however, the infant will not reach for it even after watching someone hide it (Piaget, 1937/1954). *Piaget's interpretation:* an infant who does not see an object does not know it is there. *Other possible interpretations:* The infant may know the object still exists but may not remember *where* it is. Or the infant may be distracted by other objects that *are* visible.

2. *Observation:* If we hide a toy under a clear glass, most infants will lift the glass to get the toy. If we hide it under an opaque glass, most infants will make no effort to get it. *Possible interpretation:* Infants do not ignore a covered toy because they are unable to remove the cover. They ignore it because they do not see it.

3. *Observation:* If we show an infant a toy and then turn off the lights before the infant can grab it, the infant will still reach out to grab it in the dark (Bower & Wishart, 1972). *Possible interpretation:* Contrary to the first two observations, this one seems to indicate that infants will reach for something they remember but cannot see, provided they can see nothing else. In the first two cases, objects that remain visible may distract the infant from objects that are no longer visible.

4. *Observation:* From about 9 to 11 months, an infant who watches you hide a toy will reach out to retrieve it. But if you hide the toy first on the right side and then on the left side, the infant will reach out both arms to the right side. *One interpretation:* Even at this age, infants do not fully understand that an object remains where it was hidden. *Another interpretation:* Infants know the object has been hidden but cannot remember where.

The Preoperational Stage: Early Childhood

Around age 1½ years, children reach a landmark in the intellectual development: they begin to acquire language at a rapid rate. Susan Carey (1978) has estimated that children between the ages of 1½ and 6 learn an average of nine new words *per day*—almost one new word per hour—thereby increasing their ability to tell us what they know and think (see Table 1). The fact that they can now talk about the properties of unseen objects is evidence that they have acquired the concept of object permanence. But there remain many things they do not understand at this age. For example, they have difficulty understanding that a mother can be someone else's daughter. A boy with one brother will assert that his brother has no brother. A child may say that there are more girls in a class than there are children. Piaget refers to this period as the **preoperational stage.** The child is said to lack **operations,** which are reversible mental processes. For example, for a boy to understand that his brother has a brother, he must be able to reverse the concept "having a brother."

Table 1 Conversations with Some Children at the Preoperational Stage

Q. Are you an American?

A. No, my father is an American, I'm a girl.

Q. Do you have to go to the bathroom?

A. Don't have to go. Mine peanut not working. Don't have any juice in it.

Q. Do you understand what's happening in this movie (a nature film)?

A. Yes. When the baby skunks grow up, they turn into raccoons.

Children at this age generally accept their experiences at face value. A child who sees you put a white ball behind a blue filter will say that the ball is blue. When you ask, "Yes, I know the ball looks blue, but what color is it *really?*" the child grows confused. So far as the child is concerned, any ball that *looks* blue *is* blue (Flavell, 1986).

According to Piaget, preoperational children lack the concept of conservation. Just as they fail to understand that something can still be white even if it looks blue, they fail to understand that objects conserve such properties as number, length, volume, area, and mass af-

ter the shape or arrangement of the objects has changed. They cannot perform the mental operations necessary to understand such transformations. (Table 2 shows some typical conservation tasks.)

For example, if we arrange two equal rows of pennies and ask which row contains more pennies, nearly all preoperational children will answer that the rows contain the same number of pennies. But is we spread one row out, they answer confidently that the longer row has more pennies. They do not even see a need to count the pennies to check their answer. Once we ask them to count the pennies, they discover that the number has remained the same (Gelman & Baillargeon, 1983). (Parents sometimes make use of a child's lack of conservation. A preoperational child has a cookie and asks for another one. The parent breaks the cookie in half and says, "Here. Now you have two cookies." At least some children seem satisfied.)

If we set up two glasses of the same size containing the same amount of water, and then pour the contents of one glass into a different-shaped glass, preoperational children will say that the taller, thinner glass contains more water.

I once doubted whether children really believed what they were saying in such a situation. Perhaps, I thought, the way the questions are phrased somehow tricks them into saying something they do not believe. Then something happened to convince me that preoperational children really believe their answers. One year, when I was discussing Piaget in my introductory psychology class, I invited my son Sam, then 5½ years old, to take part in a class demonstration. I started with two glasses of water, which he agreed contained equal amounts of water. Then I poured the water from one glass into a wider glass, lowering the water level. When I asked Sam which glass contained more water, he confidently pointed to the tall thin one. After class he complained, "Daddy, why did you ask me such an easy question? Everyone could see that there was more water in that glass! You should have asked me something harder to show how smart I am!"

The following year I brought Sam to class again for the same demonstration. He was now 6½ years old, about the age at which children make the transition from preoperational thinking to the next stage. I again poured the water from one of the tall glasses into a wide one and asked him which glass contained more water. He looked and paused. His face got red. Finally he whispered, "Daddy, I don't know!" After class he complained. "Why did you ask me such a hard question? I'm never coming back to any of your classes again!" The question that was embarrassingly easy a year ago had become embarrassingly difficult.

The next year, when he was 7½, I tried again. This time he answered confidently. "Both glasses have the same amount of water, of course. Why? Is this some sort of trick question?"

The Concrete-Operations Stage: Later Childhood

At about age 7, children enter the stage of concrete operations and begin to understand the conservation of physical properties. The transition is not sharp, however. The ability to understand the conservation of various properties emerges sequentially at different ages. For instance, a 6-year-old child may understand that squashing a ball of clay will not change its weight but may not realize until years later that squashing the ball will not change the volume of water it displaces when it is dropped into a glass.

The **stage of concrete operations** is Piaget's term for the stage when children can perform mental operations on concrete objects. But they still have trouble with abstract or hypothetical

ideas. For example, ask a child at this stage, "If you had five six-headed dogs, how many heads would there be?" Even a child who has no difficulty multiplying 5 times 6 is likely to object. "There is no such thing as a six-headed dog!"

Or ask this question, "How could you move a 4-mile-high mound of whipped cream from one side of the city to the other?" Older children find the question amusing and try to think of an imaginative answer. But children in the concrete-operations stage (or younger) are likely to complain that the question is silly or stupid.

Or ask, "If you could have a third eye anywhere on your body, where would you put it?" Children in this stage generally respond immediately that they would put it right between the other two, on their forehead. They seem to regard the question as not very interesting. Older children come up with more imaginative possibilities, such as on the back of their head or at the top of a finger (so they could peek around corners).

The Formal-Operations Stage: Adolescence and Adulthood

The **stage of formal operations** is Piaget's term referring to the mental processes used in dealing with abstract, hypothetical situations. Those processes demand logical, deductive reasoning and systematic planning.

Piaget set the beginning of the formal-operations stage at about age 11. He attributed some fairly sophisticated abilities to children in this stage, although later research indicates that many children take much longer to reach it and some people never do get there.

Suppose we ask three children, ages 6, 10 and 14, to arrange a set of 12 sticks in order from longest to shortest. The 6-year-old (preoperational) child fails to order the sticks correctly. The 10-year old (concrete operations) eventually gets them in the right order, but only after a

Table 2 Typical Tasks Used to Measure Conservation

Conservation of number

Preoperational children say that the two rows have the same number of pennies.

Preoperational children say that the second row has more pennies.

250cc   250cc

250cc   250cc

Conservation of volume

Preoperational children say that the two same-size containers have the same amount of water.

Preoperational children say that the taller, thinner container has more water.

Conservation of mass

Preoperational children say that the two same-size balls of clay have the same amount of clay.

Preoperational children say that a squashed ball of clay contains a different amount of clay from the same-size round ball of clay.

Conservation of mass—water displacement

A child in the early part of the concrete-operations stage may know that a round ball of clay and one that has been squashed contain the same amount of clay.

However, the same child may think that the round and the squashed balls of clay will displace different amounts of water.

great deal of trial and error. The 14-year-old (formal operations) holds the sticks upright with their bottom ends on the table and then removes the longest one, the second-longest one, and so on.

A second example: We set up five bottles of clear liquid and explain that it is possible, by mixing the liquids together in a certain combination, to produce a yellow liquid. The task is to find the right combination. Children in the concrete-operations stage plunge right in with an unsystematic trial-and-error search. They try combining bottles A and B, then C and D, them perhaps A, C, and E, and so on. By the time they work through five or six combinations they forgot which ones they have already tried. They may try one combination several times and others not at all; if and

Table 3 Summary of Piaget's Stages of Cognitive Development

Stage and approximate age	Achievements and activities	Limitations
Sensorimotor (birth to 1½ years)	Reacts to sensory stimuli through reflexes and other responses	Little use of language: seems not to understand object permanence; does not distinguish appearance from reality
Preoperational (1½ to 7 years)	Develops language; can represent objects mentally by words and other symbols; can respond to objects that are remembered but not present at the moment	Lacks operations (reversible mental processes); lacks concept of conservation; focuses on one property at a time (such as length or width), not on both at once; still has some trouble distinguishing appearance from reality
Concrete operations (7 to 11 years)	Understands conservation of mass, number, and volume; can reason logically with regard to concrete objects that can be seen or touched	Has trouble reasoning about abstract concepts and hypothetical situations
Formal operations (11 years onward)	Can reason logically about abstract and hypothetical concepts; develops strategies; plans actions in advance	None beyond the occasional irrationalities of all human thought

when they do stumble onto the correct combination, it is mostly a matter of luck.

Children in the formal-operations stage approach the problem more systematically. They may first try all the two-bottle combinations: AB, AC, AD, AE, BC, and so forth. If all those fail, they turn to three-bottle combinations: ABC, ABD, ABE, and ACD, and so on. By adopting a strategy for trying every possible combination one time and one time only, they are bound to succeed.

Children do not reach the stage of formal operations any more suddenly than they reach the concrete-operations stage. Before they can reason logically about a particular problem, they must first have had a fair amount of experi-

ence in dealing with that problem. A 9-year-old who has spent a great deal of time playing chess, reasons logically about chess problems and plans several moves ahead. The same child reverts to concrete reasoning when faced with an unfamiliar problem.

Table 3 summarizes Piaget's four stages.

SOURCE: From *Introduction to Psychology*, Second Edition, by James W. Kalat. Copyright © 1990, 1986 by Wadsworth, Inc. Pages 196–200 reprinted by permission of the publisher.

PART III

Learning from Your Computer

You learned in Parts I and II about TCDR and how to apply the critical thinking strategy to whatever you read or hear. Now we need to go one step further. The students and instructors who used the first edition of the book told us over and over how the TCDR strategy improved their success as learners and thinkers. In our many conversations with students and instructors, one question would arise: "Is there any difference in the strategies I should use when I am learning from my computer rather than a book?" The answer is no.

We have added Chapter 3 to help you learn how TCDR will serve you well as the basic thinking strategy for all of your learning. In Chapter 3, we show you how to use TCDR as you read books, journals, fiction, or nonfiction that are delivered to you on paper or electronically. It really makes no difference to you how you receive the information. What is important is how you approach thinking about and learning information, whenever and however it comes to you.

Questions You Will Be Able to Answer after Reading "Learning from Your Computer"

Why will I be able to learn more successfully after reading this information?

Why should I use the same learning strategies whether I am reading information on a computer or from a textbook?

How do the learning styles of more successful and less successful learners differ?

Why should I always study as though I were practicing to take a test?

When I use computers or books, what are the best strategies for test preparation?

What do good questions and answers look like?

What is the best reading strategy for me when I read from a computer or book?

What inefficient reading and learning strategies must I eliminate to be a successful learner?

How will the TCDR strategy of thinking improve my ability to develop good questions and answers?

How can I use TCDR as I read from my computer or book?

Why should I always develop questions before I read?

Why don't most people think about developing a learning strategy?

What are the three reasons question-and-answer learning techniques will make me a more successful thinker and learner?

LEARNING FROM YOUR COMPUTER
NEED NOT BE A PROBLEM

The computer age presents you with a series of challenges you may have never faced. Like it or not, you may take courses in which the only information you receive comes from your computer, whether you use a desktop, laptop, handheld, PDA (Personal Digital Assistant), or dedicated e-book hardware device. There are many electronic book formats available, from text downloaded onto a computer or PDA to be read with reader software to books available for use online through a Web browser or through a dedicated e-book hardware device. Publishers are scrambling to have their content available in a wide array of these formats. The variety works to your advantage because you can easily experiment with various formats, pick your favorite, and then use the power of the computer to learn more effectively.

If you take online courses, or even traditional courses, you may find yourself without books, notes, or course presentations to mark or study. All you may have is the information on your computer screen. Is this a problem? Some people may make it a problem or an excuse for poor learning, but you don't have to. In fact, you can learn better than ever if you spend the next hour thinking about how you can use the strategies that follow for learning from computers as well as books.

QUESTIONS YOU NEED TO ASK ABOUT
USING YOUR COMPUTER

To learn successfully from computers, you need to ask yourself a few basic questions: What do I want to accomplish by using the information on the computer? Do I want to learn and remember information that, before computers, would have been unavailable to me? Do I want to learn information that will allow me to do things that might not have been possible before computers? Will my computer skills help me become more successful in the future?

These are important questions, and embedded in them is a concern that many students express: How can I use computers to be more successful in high school and college? The following are some questions students often ask.

How do I learn to use the information available on my computer to be a better student?

How can I use computers to be more successful on tests?

When students use computers to prepare for tests, how is what successful learners do different from what less successful learners do?

How can I be successful when the only information I have for preparing for my tests is from a computer?

How can I be successful on my tests when I don't have paper books, articles, and course notes from which to study?

How can I sit in front of a computer for hours and learn?

How do I compare my ideas about the test questions with the ideas of other students when I don't have classmates with whom to discuss upcoming tests?

These are excellent questions, all of which you will find answers for as you read on.

For most students, performing well on tests is very important, although scoring well on tests is not the only reason you will need to learn from a computer. Still, we have never met a student who didn't want to do well on tests, so learning to use the computer to enhance test performance is one of the most valuable skills we can teach you.

THE END PRODUCT: WHAT IS IT YOU WANT TO ACHIEVE AS YOU LEARN FROM YOUR COMPUTER?

Have you ever taken a test that didn't involve answering questions? Some tests don't ask explicit questions. For example, you might be asked to play a Beethoven piano concerto or run a 100-meter dash. These are performance tests. However, even during a performance test (or while practicing for it), you constantly monitor and assess your performance by asking yourself whether you are doing the right things. The questions you generate keep your performance moving in the proper direction and are critical to the learning process. Both performance tests and written tests require you to ask and answer intelligent questions. As you use your computer, you should also be conscious of how well you are developing and answering potential test questions.

Learning and performing are closely related. You learn so that you can perform, and as you perform, you learn about what you are doing well and what you need to improve. To learn successfully and perform well using a computer, you need to identify the end product and determine how to use the computer to achieve that end product.

The end product for successful learners is demonstrating that they can answer important questions raised by the information they have been asked to learn. Successful learners know how to gather the necessary information and identify potential questions so that they can provide the correct answers in various testing situations. In other words, successful students must be expert test takers.

Your ability to convince your instructor and yourself that you have understood the material is based on your ability to answer questions in class orally, in written assignments, or on tests. Although other factors may contribute to success in a course, the most critical tool in successful learning and high performance is a strategy for developing great questions and answers.

How do you learn to develop those great questions and answers from the information you get from your computer? To answer this question, we will simulate a learning situation that takes place thousands of times a day.

SIMULATING A COMPUTER-LEARNING EXPERIENCE

As you read this, imagine that you are sitting in front of a computer. Imagine also that you are learning the way commercial airplane pilots learn. Pretend you are a student pilot in a flight simulator. When you enter the simulator, you have several goals. Your long-term goal is to fly a plane. Your short-term goal is to demonstrate that you can complete the instructional tasks for the session. This exercise is similar to demonstrating to your violin instructor that you can perform a piece of music properly or showing your history or math instructor that you can answer questions or complete problems correctly.

During your session in the flight simulator, you are tested on concepts relevant to flying a plane under a particular set of circumstances. Your answers to conceptual questions about what you would do in different situations to operate the plane demonstrate whether you can perform procedural operations in the cockpit, such as taking off, flying, and landing. The airline expects you to learn from information delivered to a computer. Thus, you spend many hours answering questions and performing tasks in the flight simulator before you ever enter the cockpit of a plane for an actual practice run. There is no way any airline would put you aboard a commercial carrier unless you had demonstrated on many occasions in flight simulation that you could successfully answer every possible question about operating the plane. After all, if you become a pilot, you will have many people's lives in your hands.

Most of us probably feel mentally fatigued just thinking about all the flight simulation training that pilots go through. Compare this to what you will do as a student day after day, year after year, as you train to become a successful learner. You'll be working just as hard, if not harder. Think about the number of questions you'll have to answer to pass the many tests that you'll take to earn your degree or certificate. Don't panic! Millions of students have done well in college using the strategies you are going to learn.

For some of you, it is not just a question of doing well. To get into many programs, colleges, and graduate schools, you have to score *exceptionally* well. You can't afford to be merely a good learner; you have to be a great learner. To be a great learner, you have to do what pilots do: teach yourself how to enter the learning simulator and perform exceedingly well. So let's get to it. How will you interact with your computer? What strategies will you use to learn as much as you want and score the highest possible score on *any* test.

Where Do I Start?

What is your end goal as you learn information obtained on your computer? We have posed this question to several thousand successful students. When we compile their answers, we find that students want several outcomes, but two items top the list: They want to learn important information, and they want to do well on their tests. We suspect that you want the same outcomes, no doubt for the same reasons. When you eventually achieve these outcomes, you'll graduate from college, go on to a successful career, and live happily ever after. Some would call this the American dream. We would suggest it is the behavior pattern of intelligent people worldwide. A diploma is the key to financial and social mobility, so if your bottom line includes success in your course work, then you need to start by improving your learning skills and doing well on tests.

PRINCIPLES OF SUCCESS

By studying the behavior of successful students, we have found that most of them follow four basic principles:

Principle I: Read and Study to Pass Tests

Principle II: Ask Intelligent Questions

Principle III: Anticipate Your Instructor's Questions

Principle IV: Develop Good Answers

Successful students have chosen to adapt these principles as they learn information from their computers. It is no longer possible for successful students to receive all the information they need from traditional textbooks, works of fiction and nonfiction, journal articles, course notes, and study-group sessions. The information successful learners read and understand is now often delivered electronically; there is no paper to write on, no printed book to annotate or highlight, and no binder to hold course notes. So how do good learners use these principles with the computer?

Successful students do what successful students are known to do: They analyze the problem and adapt. Here is a condensed version of one very successful student's description of the learning process:

> *When I talk with my friends about what we have to do to succeed, no matter what else you believe, the bottom line is that we have to ask and answer good questions. We ask and answer questions when writing papers, reading books, taking notes, talking with friends, participating in class, and taking tests. So now, when I have to get my test questions and answers from the computer, I do what I always do. I take the information from the screen and turn it into questions and answers. What I don't do is try to memorize the information. I write out questions from all the information I see on the computer and then I find the answers. Sometimes the answers are in the book or article I am reading on the computer. Often, I have to go to other sources of information to find a complete answer. One thing I learned is that just because a question is discussed in a book doesn't mean you will always find a complete answer. That is why instructors suggest reference books.*

Other students said:

> *Computers have created a problem for me. I still need to turn information on my computer screen into questions and answers. That isn't always easy, because I can't always download it. I can't mark it up on the computer screen. I have to take notes from the screen that are turned into questions and answers. The only thing that has changed is that now I have to manipulate electronically delivered information versus information that I could hold in my hand or carry around in my backpack. Now I have to be able to sit in front of a computer and do much more than just read information. I have to rearrange that information on the computer into questions and answers.*

> *Many other students I see are struggling and still not getting the point. You can't read and memorize everything you read on the computer. You can't read and remember everything that passes before your eyes on a screen. You have to turn the information into something useful.*

YOUR STRATEGY FOR USING THE FOUR PRINCIPLES OF SUCCESS

Reading and studying to pass tests, asking intelligent questions, and anticipating your instructors' questions are strategies that are part of a system of learning. As you sit in front of your computer, you'll need an overall strategy for manipulating the information—you'll need to read the information and turn it into questions and answers. We will teach you a system of reading and learning that will help you achieve two important goals: learning important information and doing well on tests.

This system of learning asks you to consider dumping certain bad habits you may have:

Reading as though you can memorize what you are reading

Reading slowly

Reading everything placed before your eyes

In an attempt to convince you to change these habits, we could present you with a wealth of research on efficient and effective strategies for reading and learning. Instead, we ask you to try one of the exercises that follow.

EXERCISE 1

If we gave you an hour to memorize a 25-page chapter in a history textbook and then offered you a million dollars to repeat everything you had read without referring to the chapter, could you do it? We have never met anyone who could. No one can remember everything they have read.

In contrast, if we gave you ten questions about the chapter and then gave you an hour to read it and look for the answers, what would be the result? We've done this exercise hundreds of times. When students look at ten questions before reading a chapter and then look for the answers while they read, the result is predictable. At the end of the hour, students still cannot repeat word for word what is in the chapter. They can, however, give a fairly complete answer to each of the ten questions, using their own words.

Give it a try. Take any textbook chapter and find ten questions (usually located at the end of the chapter or at the beginning in the chapter objectives). If the chapter doesn't have chapter questions or objectives, take ten minutes and survey the chapter. Make up questions by reviewing chapter and paragraph headings, italicized words, and other important-looking information. Write the questions down and review them. Then, with the goal of answering the questions, take an hour to read the chapter. While you are reading, feel free to stop and write answers to the questions—or you can wait until you have completed the chapter to write your answers. Either way, don't hesitate to refer to the text as you write.

What's the result? After reading the chapter, you'll be able to answer the questions. Isn't that a great surprise? We don't mean to be glib, but it does surprise some students that, once they finish reading, they can answer the questions fairly quickly.

How does what you just did differ from what most students do? Most students pick up the book and begin reading the chapter. What's the matter with this? Nothing, if you don't want to have a good understanding of what you have read after you finish.

When students just read a chapter, they don't have any direction. They don't know what they should have accomplished once they have finished the chapter. When you ask such students what the first words were that entered their mind when they finished reading (assuming they didn't fall asleep), typical responses are:

What did I just read?

Thank goodness I'm finished.

I'll probably have to read this again to make sure I know what the chapter is about.

I am not sure what I've learned!

I wonder what will be on the test from this chapter?

EXERCISE 2

Ask a friend to name a recent book he or she has read. Once your friend names the book, ask that person if he or she can repeat word for word what is on any page of the book. Offer this person a million dollars to do so. Your friend won't be able to remember every word.

Then ask your friend to list some important questions that were answered in the book and give the answers. Your friend *will* be able to do this.

What you will see from this exercise is that no one remembers what they have read word for word, or even close to it. People remember only important information—ideas, concepts, definitions, emotional issues, and so on.

The exercises illustrate that people remember answers to questions. Indeed, this is how people think, in logical constructs or relationships such as linked questions and answers.

People spend their lives looking for answers to questions. The questioning process is the way people pursue knowledge. If you look at or listen to information without using the three learning strategies that follow, you set yourself up to learn in an inefficient way. We're not saying you wouldn't learn the principles, but these strategies do make learning more effective and efficient, as well as painless and fun.

Strategy 1

Know What Questions You Want to Answer before You Read

Strategy 2

Read Looking for Answers to Questions

Strategy 3

Answer Your Questions as You Read

HOW TO USE YOUR COMPUTER TO FIND
QUESTIONS AND TO DEVELOP ANSWERS

Let's recap how you are going to learn from your computer the information you need to do well on tests. What we know is that you'll be looking for questions and answers as you read.

What type of information will you be reading? Most students will be reviewing textbook chapters, journal articles, fiction and nonfiction books, and course notes. Your instructor, a book publisher, or special Internet provider will make the information available to you.

Will you use the same strategies for reading all these materials? Yes, you will always be reading with the ultimate goal of doing well on the test, which means you'll always be looking for questions and answers. With some minor variations, the strategy for reading will be the same no matter how the information is formatted. To develop useful questions and answers, you need to employ two other strategies. First, figure out what intelligent questions are. Second, anticipate your instructor's questions. Your instructors are intelligent people who are experts in their fields, so it's likely that the questions they ask you in class, in handouts, and from the books and articles they assign will be intelligent questions.

One difference we've found between good and very good learners is that very good learners not only know how to develop good questions, they know how to respond with good answers. So, let us show you how to use the information available through your computer to develop those great questions and answers. Let's start with the questions.

SITUATION

You are taking a computer-based course in a social science. In this course, you must take several multiple-choice tests. All the written information you need comes from an electronic textbook. You can't print the information, however, so you must learn without having the information on paper.

What is the difference between this scenario and a traditional course in which you have a printed textbook and course notes? Seemingly, a lot. You can't annotate or highlight your book; you can't lay the book out on your desk or take it to the library. You must work at home on your computer or in a computer station at your college. But is the end product any different? No, you still have to pass the test. So what will you do? Consider the following approach.

DEVELOP YOUR QUESTIONS BY
SURVEYING YOUR CHAPTER

The goal of surveying is to determine what questions the chapter answers and where to find the answers to the most important questions. Once you know what your questions are, all you have to do is develop good answers. Remember, you aren't memorizing the chapter. You won't be taking a test that requires you to write the chapter word for word; instructors always ask you to answer questions. Whenever you find yourself reverting to the old strategy of reading slowly to try to remember the text, force yourself to stop!

STEP 1: SURVEY AND QUESTION

Go to the beginning and end of the chapter to see whether there is a list of chapter objectives, a list of questions, or a chapter summary. Whichever of these you find, read them to start. Once you have read them, you'll be able to develop a list of questions you think will be on your test. If you don't find these questions, take a few minutes to skim the chapter looking at paragraph headings and key words. You can formulate questions from this information.

You can then move between the chapter and another location on your computer where you have written the questions on which you want to focus. Developing this list of questions is critical. It forces you to think seriously about what you think your instructor views as important. We are trying to get you to think like your instructor—the expert—and to anticipate his or her questions. You can always revise this list later, when you read the chapter.

Now that you have established "advanced organizers" (questions that organize your thinking about the chapter), you'll need to survey the chapter. Surveying the chapter means skimming it to locate information pertaining to the questions you have predicted and also to find any additional questions that might be important to consider. As you survey, look at the headings, subheadings, illustrations, pictures, charts, italicized words, and definitions in the margin.

This process should not be so long or drawn out that it tires you before you start reading. Your survey might take all of ten minutes. During the survey, you'll probably find a few more questions not mentioned in the chapter objectives, questions, or summary. Take a minute or two to add these to your list.

Where are you now? You have read the chapter objectives, summary, and questions. You have also surveyed the chapter and come up with additional questions.

Why Is This 15–20 Minutes Spent Developing Questions So Valuable?

You will find that reading the chapter summary, questions, or objectives establishes a clear focus for your reading. By surveying the chapter, you narrow your focus even further, refining and adding to your questions. Surveying also reduces your anxiety by targeting the location of the answers to your questions. Your reading is no longer directionless. You know what you're looking for, and now you can go after the answers.

STEP 2: READ TO ANSWER QUESTIONS AND ANSWER THE QUESTIONS

Read as quickly as you can to find the answers to the questions you've developed. When you're looking for information that answers your questions, you're reading selectively. When you come to a section of information that answers a question, you slow down and pay careful attention to the most important points.

As you find answers to questions, you have two options. You can stop reading each time you find an answer to a question and write it down. This option is helpful for those students who don't want to wait until they complete the chapter before answering their questions. Other students prefer to slow down, think through the answers, and then continue reading.

Once they have completed all the reading, they go back and write out their answers.

Either strategy works. Do whichever makes you most comfortable. You may be familiar with other reading strategies that rely on your reading at a constant rate. Our strategy encourages you to read rapidly to find important information, answers to your questions. When you come to the information, you make sure you understand it by shaping the information into a coherent answer. Then you begin reading again.

You will periodically come to information that responds to a question you haven't predicted. Slow down. Develop a new question, answer the question, and start reading again.

When you find information that answers a question, you need to restructure the information into an answer that makes sense to you. This step is critical to the entire reading process. Later, we'll talk about what a good answer looks like.

STEP 3: WRITE AND RECITE YOUR ANSWERS

If you did not write answers to your questions while you were reading, do this now.

If you want to remember important information, you have to practice using it the way it will be used on a test. In your courses, you are constantly asked to answer questions, whether orally or in writing, so you must be comfortable providing answers both ways.

Once you've used your computer to record the answers to your questions, you then have two options for checking how well you have learned the material. You have your list of questions and answers saved on your computer, and you also have the chapter available. You want to make sure you can write answers to your questions and also talk about them. You should constantly quiz yourself by writing and speaking the answers.

You should not, however, read and reread the chapter. No one is going to ask you to write or recite the text. Instead, your instructor will ask you to answer questions on paper or out loud.

A big difference between American students and European students is that European students spend a lot of time talking out answers. These students practice answering questions orally. Why? Schools and colleges in Great Britain and Western Europe focus on oral presentations. These educational systems often live by the motto, "If you can't say it, you don't know it!" We want you to be just as good—that is why we're urging you to formulate both written and oral answers.

STEP 4: REVIEW

Now that you have a set of questions and answers, you can be confident that you know what the chapter is about. You won't need to worry about whether you are prepared for the exam or whether you should reread the chapter or memorize it.

You will be the owner of a solid set of answers to the important questions from the text. You know that you may be quizzed orally in class, but you're ready for that. You're prepared for the written test too, because you have practiced the exact behavior that will be required of you. You have no reason to fear or panic. Panic is the result of poor preparation. Skilled preparation reassures people that no matter what questions are thrown at them, they will have a very good chance of answering successfully.

This strategy of learning allows you to get test anxiety out of your life. You know what is expected of you, and you have prepared with a game plan. When you see your instructor's test questions, they may not be exactly what you predicted, but the odds are that the questions and answers you have developed are similar enough to those on the test that you will do well.

We have spent many years teaching this strategy, and the results have been clear. Students who prepare for tests by developing test questions learn a great deal and do well on tests. Those who prepare for tests in other ways often do all right, but they will have spent far too much time studying and preparing in ways that are inefficient and painful.

Think about all the centers that have opened up in the last twenty years to help students improve in school or do well on standardized tests. The programs that Peterson's, Kaplan, or the Princeton Review have developed share a major premise. They claim to be able to improve scores on the ACT, SAT, GRE, MCAT, and so on by teaching you how to take tests. Their primary strategy is teaching you the types of question that will appear on the test and how to improve your skills at answering them.

Is their approach anti-intellectual or antilearning? Not by a long shot. These folks realize that the students who want to do well in school, whether high school or college, may have had inadequate preparation in test taking. From their perspective, it is not a question of whether people are smart; rather, they recognize that students have been taught inefficient ways of learning.

So far, we have focused primarily on the strategies for developing good questions. Now it's time to consider the "missing link."

THE MISSING LINK: WHAT DO GOOD QUESTIONS AND ANSWERS LOOK LIKE?

Most students have a good idea of the types of question they'll be asked to answer. Common types will ask you to:

Compare and contrast . . .

Interpret the following . . .

Describe the structure of . . .

Discuss the relationship between . . .

List and describe the important . . .

Give several examples of . . .

Choose an example of . . .

Describe the function of . . .

Why does . . .

Identify the following . . .

Most students don't have difficulty developing questions if they take the time to do so. Textbooks are loaded with questions. Many introductory courses even have student study guides or lab manuals that are full of practice questions and exercises.

In contrast, textbooks seldom provide satisfactory models for answers to essay questions. Instructors expect students to be able to develop those answers by reading the book and pulling together the relevant information. When was the last time an instructor provided you with sample answers to essay questions? Or the last time an instructor provided you not only with sample answers but also with models showing the differences between *A, B, C, D,* and *F* answers?

Many English instructors define for students what they expect in a paper and often give detailed descriptions of the characteristics of a good paper. Some instructors will even provide models of *A, B, C, D,* and *F* papers and will work with you to understand the differences between them.

Other instructors may provide models of what they expect in research papers, lab reports, and other assignments. But few will give you clear examples of what good answers look like.

Developing Answers for Your Questions

WHAT DO WE WANT YOU TO LEARN?

The end goal is to teach you how to use the TCDR strategy to organize information found on your computer into good answers. TCDR will help you develop excellent answers. As you use this strategy, you will find that your learning and thinking capacities are enhanced when you practice developing questions and answers.

As Parts I and II have shown, TCDR strategy teaches you to think and learn by looking at information in a way that increases your ability to focus, organize, categorize, process, and retrieve the information. You think and learn in more logical ways and will be better equipped to make sense of information that previously seemed complex or difficult to understand. The end result of learning TCDR is an improved ability to answer questions comprehensively.

HOW DOES TCDR WORK WITH COMPUTER INFORMATION?

Recall that the entire TCDR strategy is a simple process with four basic components: topic, class, description, and relevance.

As you read from your computer screen, looking for the answer to a question, you identify the information that fits these categories by asking the following questions:

What is the *topic* I must understand?

What is the *class* to which this topic belongs?

What is the *description* of the topic?

What is the *relevance* of the topic?

We found that the answers that earned students a grade of *B* or better typically included a statement about the topic, a reference to its class, and a description and discussion of its relevance.

Students we interviewed described a process by which they read the information while seeking answers to questions. Once students identified the questions they needed to answer, they scanned the information, looking for data that fit these four categories. Good students recognized that at a minimum they had to include a statement about the topic or topics that were pertinent to their answers. Describing the class to which these topics belonged was important because it helped define the topic. Every good answer went on to describe the topic and discuss its relevance or importance.

Using TCDR

HOW DO I USE TCDR ON A DAILY BASIS?

Whenever you read information on your computer, you are seeking answers to questions. When you use TCDR to find the critical information for your answers, the questions you ask include:

What Is the Topic I Must Understand?

What are the key topics of the chapter as a whole?

What are the key topics of the page I am reading now?

What Is the Overall Class to Which This Topic Belongs?

What is the whole of which this topic is a part?

What is the main heading under which this topic appears?

What Is the Description of the Topic?

What are the characteristics, features, and properties of the topic?

What does this topic look like?

How would you describe the topic so that someone else could recognize it, whether in reading material, audio material, or real life?

What Is the Relevance of the Topic?

What is importance of the topic to you, to other people, or to some other topic you are considering?

Why has the topic been introduced?

What role does the topic play in understanding or explaining other things?

How does the topic affect other things?

Take, for example, the great African-American boxer, leader, poet, and humanitarian, a man of strong social conscience, Muhammad Ali. If you were seeking information about Ali via computer, how you frame your questions would in turn clearly define the reading process.

You would think about Ali as your *topic.* Narrowing the focus to a particular *class* (boxer, leader, poet, humanitarian, African American, or man of social conscience) dramatically alters the information you will seek to *describe* Ali and discuss his *relevance.* For example, describing Ali as a man of social conscience would be very different from describing his role in the sport of boxing. Additionally, the arenas in which his work as a social reformer and his role as a boxer are relevant will be different. Thus, it is very important to distinguish the class of the topic and put the information on description and relevance in proper perspective.

Your information search will focus on gathering the information necessary to answer your questions about *topic, class, description,* and *relevance.*

The concept of TCDR is simple. TCDR represents the observation of several thousand students who were able to successfully look at information and organize it into a logical framework. No student ever said to us, "I use TCDR." Rather, we asked them what they did as they sought information to answer questions.

As a group, these students had a clear model of the minimum information they needed to supply a good answer. How did they come to this conclusion? In our system of education it is likely that instructors look for TCDR features in answers to questions, which, in turn, encourages students to use this strategy to develop their answers.

Successful students also compare and contrast answers that earned them excellent grades with answers that earned them lower grades. This is the process of every successful scholar, performer, or athlete. We analyze actions that lead to success and those that result in mistakes. Over time, our behavior is shaped by its consequences.

If you interview scholars, performers, and athletes, asking them what they do in different situations to succeed, you will find that great scientists can describe in detail the steps they follow in the process of inquiry and research, just as great ballerinas can describe in detail how they practice and perform. Likewise, Jack Nicklaus and Tiger Woods can describe in detail what they do in different golfing situations. Those of us who are less successful on the golf course need to study the masters if we want to be able answer questions like "Why did I slice the ball?"

WHAT IS THE LESSON?

Every time you turn on your computer, you should be asking three questions:

Where am I going?

How will I get there?

How will I know when I have arrived?

You'll know where you are going by asking yourself, "What questions do I want and need to answer?" You'll know how you're going to get there, by seeking information that answers your questions. You'll know you have arrived when you find answers to your questions and prove to yourself that you know them by writing and speaking them out.

DID YOU KNOW?

Did you know that most college textbook publishers have quizzes and tests on their Web sites, usually specific to the book you are using in class? This means that publishers have provided you with questions and answers to help you study for tests. What better way to study for a test than to practice taking a test on your book's subject matter? The publisher has probably printed the URL for its Web site somewhere in your book or on its cover. Go to the site and look through the student resources for questions related to your book or its subject matter.

DID YOU KNOW?

Did you know that publishers of most electronic textbooks have linked study and review questions to the place in the e-book where the answers can be found? Publishers also often link key terms, footnotes, and icons in the margin to help students navigate the chapter. So click around on your e-book and find answers you may not have known were there. Most e-books also have some search capabilities. You may use the search feature to find key words that can help you answer questions you have formulated for studying purposes. You can't do these things with a printed book; hyperlinks and search functions are added features of e-books that you can use to your advantage.

LEARNING FROM PROFESSIONAL JOURNALS

Many journals are now available on the Internet. Journals typically create problems for readers because of their complexity. Journal articles are written by professors, doctors, and researchers for other professors, doctors, and researchers, not for the average undergraduate college student. Nevertheless, students have nothing to fear: When you download a journal article, you'll follow a process similar to the one you've learned for developing and finding answers to questions from textbooks.

Read the Abstract and Summary

Your goal is to answer questions about the article. So, what should you read first to develop your questions? Journal articles are often preceded by an *abstract,* a summary of the article's main points. An abstract typically helps you formulate the author's questions and answers. Thus, the abstract does your work for you, giving you the important questions and briefly summarizing the answers. In some cases, you need read no further. You have your answers in brief and you can proceed to another article.

If you want to leave the article with some confidence that you really understand the answers, you should probably go to the end of the article. The summary or conclusion often repeats what is said in the abstract, possibly expanding on other questions that were important but not critical enough to be noted at the start. In most cases, you'll find any additional information you might need.

The remainder of most articles consists of the introduction, methods, and results sections. Depending on what your instructor wants you to know, you may also need to answer questions about the researchers' methodology and their strategies for analyzing the data. Any reader working at a higher level in a field will need to determine the questions that should be answered in these sections. For most of you, however, the abstract and conclusion will provide your starting and finishing point. The other sections may confuse rather than clarify the discussion for you, especially if you lack expertise in scientific methodology and statistical analysis. Even so, you will be able to answer several critical questions about the researchers' inquiry and their conclusions.

WHERE SHOULD YOU KEEP THESE QUESTIONS AND ANSWERS?

Many students like to keep a journal or log on their computer. As these students read articles, they answer questions about each article in a journal. When they review for a test, rather than reread the journal abstracts, they consult their journal for the answers to the questions from each article. Clearly, this review method is much faster than rereading each abstract.

Think of the time it would take to download each journal article and read each abstract again. With a log of answers to questions, you'll spend less time reading and reviewing. Most important, you'll practice asking and answering questions about the articles you've read.

LEARNING FROM BOOKS OF FICTION AND NONFICTION

Many students look at a book of several hundred pages and wonder, "How am I going to have time to read this, let alone understand it?" A nontextbook doesn't have the typical advanced organizers or learning aids. Such a book seldom has chapter summaries, lists of questions, or chapter objectives. But don't worry, you can still use the same strategies.

Surveying and Questioning

You can survey the book by first reading the front and back covers. Read the introduction and skim through the table of contents to get a sense of the important questions answered in the book.

WHAT ARE GOOD QUESTIONS FOR FICTION AND NONFICTION BOOKS?

The list of possible questions is endless. Your main concern is to develop a few questions on which to focus when you begin. Not only will your questions help you focus, they will help keep you awake. As you read, you'll discover new topics and questions you hadn't predicted. Whether you are reading a biography of John F. Kennedy or a classic Hemingway tale, your questions will allow you to read rapidly as you seek answers. Without a focus, your mind will wander and you'll read more slowly.

Here are a few standard questions you might ask:

Who are the main characters in the story?

How are the characters related to one another?

Who is the narrator of the story?

What is the plot?

What are the subplots?

Is this work characteristic of the author's work?

Is the author taking a particular position?

What information does the author use to support his/her position?

What are the critical ideas or issues that the author is raising?

Reading

Once you have surveyed the book and developed questions, read each chapter. After finishing the first few chapters, ask yourself, "Is this book asking and answering the same questions I thought it would?"

As you proceed through the work, you can move back and forth between the text and your computer notes. After every few chapters, summarize what you've read. The end product will be a two- or three-page summary of the book.

Ensure that your summary is not a retelling of the book. Rather, your summary should answer specific questions about key points that you, the author, and your instructor have raised. Most instructors are very clear about the information they want you to look for as you read works of fiction and nonfiction.

The problem many readers face when trying to read works of fiction or nonfiction is that they try to read slowly and remember everything. Your goal is to remember the major ideas presented. You want to be able to understand the book's strengths and weaknesses, discuss issues raised by the author, debate positions taken, list reasons you liked or disliked specific statements, and quiz yourself and your friends over what took place in the book. You'll do this best if you read rapidly, looking for the answers to your questions.

THE PSYCHOLOGY BEHIND LEARNING TO LEARN

Before the large-scale introduction of personal computers in the late 1970s and the Internet in the late 1980s, much research was done on human learning and thinking. By the early 1980s, we knew a lot about the strategies that successful students use to learn from traditional texts, written materials, and lectures. The strategies students have used so successfully with printed books and journals work just as well for learning information from computers for several reasons.

Reason 1

When you know the information you are looking for, you are more likely to find it.

Analogy: When you develop questions before you read, you are more likely to find answers to those questions than if you start without questions.

Reason 2

When you know the information for which you are looking, you are more likely to stay awake and find what you want.

Analogy: If you develop questions before you read, you will stay alert and find answers. If you read aimlessly, with no questions in mind, you will become bored, learn less, and possibly fall asleep.

Reason 3

When you know the information you are looking for, you will feel rewarded and energized when you find it.

Analogy: If you establish questions and read to find the answers, every time you find an answer, you'll have the "Ah Ha" feeling. You'll feel energized and keep looking for more answers. If you don't have questions, you can't be rewarded, because you never find answers, and you'll feel unsure of what you have learned.

CONCLUSION

Today, the challenges we face as we apply the principles of learning and thinking to computer-based systems can easily be met. The strategies for learning from a computer are the same as those used for printed books, notes, and journals. With computer-based learning, all that is really different is that now you must sit with your computer and manipulate the information into questions, answers, and summaries of what you have learned. Although electronic tools alter the way in which information is delivered as well as the amount of information you receive, the end product is the same.

Eventually, you will be able to plug into information systems from almost anywhere in the world. To keep up with changes in how information is delivered, you will need to learn how to operate ever-more advanced forms of computers and handheld devices. You should be able, however, to use new technology efficiently and effectively for learning if you follow the strategies we have presented.

For those of you who want to know more about successful learning, we recommend:

Student Success: How to Succeed in College and Still Have Time for Your Friends by Timothy L. Walter, Al Siebert, and Laurence N. Smith, 8th ed. (Fort Worth: Harcourt Brace, 2000).

The Adult Learner's Guide to College Success by Laurence N. Smith and Timothy L. Walter, 2d ed. (Belmont, Calif.: Wadsworth, 1997).

Critical Thinking: Building the Basics

Part I—Answer Key

Page Number	Exercise Number	Answers (and Comments)
4		topic–chair; class–a piece of furniture; description–consisting of a flat surface supported by three or more legs; relevance–used for sitting on
6	1	1st answer bad; missing: full description of appearance
6	2	2nd answer bad; missing: relevance (doesn't tell what they are used for)
7	3	1st answer bad; missing: class (animal)
7	4	2nd answer bad; missing: description ("signed by King John" is the only description provided in the passage)
7	5	2nd answer bad; missing: relevance (the purpose was to limit the king's power)
7	6	1st answer bad; missing: class (It is classified here as a document and not, for example, as a law or command or decree.)
8	7	1st answer bad; missing: description ("heavy and dark orange")
8	8	1st answer bad; missing: relevance (does not tell what it is used for)
8	9	2nd answer bad; missing: class (does not tell whether it is a liquid or a solid or a chemical, and so on)

Page Number	Exercise Number	Answers (and Comments)
8	10	1. salmon 2. seafood, or fish 3. live in the sea; lay eggs in quite freshwater streams, which they reach by swimming upstream from the sea 4. used as food for people
9	11	1. bad 2. class 3. for example: "Iodine is a chemical that is contained in sea water, kelp and shellfish. It has a silvery-gray and flaky appearance. It is used as an antiseptic."
9	12	1 bad 2. description 3. for example: "Rain is a form of moisture made up of billions of tiny droplets, which, when they get too heavy in the clouds, are pulled by gravity to the earth. Rain is essential for the life and growth of plants and animals."
10	1	topic
10	2	class
11	3	topic
11	4	topic
11	5	class
11	6	class
11	7	salmon 1, trout 2, rainbow trout 3, steelhead 4
11	8	class
12	9	topic
12	10	class

Page Number	Exercise Number	Answers (and Comments)
12	1	example (topic)
12	2	relevance
12	3	description
13	4	class
13	5	topic
13	6	relevance
13	7	relevance
13	8	class
13	9	class
14	10	topic
14	11	class
14	12	description
14	13	relevance
14	14	relevance
14	15	relevance
14	16	topic
15	17	topic
15	18	description
15	19	topic
15	20	topic
15	21	relevance
15	22	topic
16	1	What is it about?
16	2	What is a general name?
16	3	What does it look like?
16	4	What is it used for?
16	5	What is it about?
16	6	What are its characteristics?
16	7	Is it possibly a process or a method?
16	8	What is its purpose?
17	9	What happens first? What next?
17	10	Why is it important?

Page Number	Exercise Number	Answers (and Comments)
17	1	description
17	2	description
17	3	relevance
17	4	relevance
17	5	relevance

Note: We hope that you realized that the main topic is power and the social sciences. The practice items below examine some of the topics that support the main topic.

19	1	

What is the topic?

social science

What is the class?

Not stated in this excerpt—but social science is one of the three traditional divisions of academic study, together with the natural sciences and the humanities.

What is the description?

The study of human behavior; has several separate "disciplines" such as anthropology, sociology, economics, psychology, political science and history, and each use different concepts, methods, and data in their studies of behavior.

What is the relevance?

—to provide explanations of various aspects of human behavior

—"to contribute to an understanding of the forces that modify the conduct of individuals, control their behavior, and shape their lives."

Page Number	**Exercise Number**	**Answers (and Comments)**

19   2

<u>What is the topic?</u>
anthropology

<u>What is the class?</u>
social science

<u>What is the description?</u>
—In general, the study of people and their ways of life.
—Specifically, the study of (1) people's biological and physical characteristics and (2) the ways of life of both ancient and modern peoples.

<u>What is the relevance?</u>
—the overall topic of power will be examined from the perspective of each of the separate disciplines, in this case, anthropology.

19   3

<u>What is the topic?</u>
cultural anthropology

(Note: This is only a briefly mentioned topic, and should not distract the reader from the larger topic, anthropology, which is a subtopic under the broad topic of power.)

<u>What is the class?</u>
anthropology

<u>What is the description?</u>
the study of the ways of life of both ancient and modern peoples

<u>What is the relevance?</u>
—to better define anthropology
—to set the scene for the next topic, culture.

Page Number	Exercise Number	Answers (and Comments)
20	4	**What is the topic?** sociology **What is the class?** a social science **What is the description?** the study of relationships among individuals and groups (All of the information in the paragraph describes what sociology studies.) **What is the relevance?** *same as for anthropology, above*
20	5	**What is the topic?** stratification **What is the class?** a classification system **What is the description?** a system of classifying people according to their "ranking," which is determined by how people make their living, the control they have over the livings of others **What is the relevance?** a person's rank (in a stratification system) influences the amount of power he or she has (Remember: the main topic in this passage is power.)
22	1	**What is the topic?** comet **What is the class?** bodies in the solar system

Page Number	Exercise Number	**Answers (and Comments)**

<u>What is the description?</u>

—comets are small bodies in the solar system; visible among the stars; seem motionless to naked eye (they do not flash like shooting stars)

—have several parts: comet head, comet tail, and comet nucleus (See topic next page.)

<u>What is the relevance?</u>

To answer this you would need access either to the end of this passage on comets or to the rest of the chapter.

23   2   What other topics that are equivalent to comets would you expect to find in this chapter?

other bodies in the solar system

23   3   <u>What is the topic?</u>
comet nucleus

<u>What is the class?</u>

comets, or comet parts, or composition of a comet

<u>What is the description?</u>

—located at the center of the bright starlike point at the center of the comet head

—only solid part of the comet; a worldlet of dirty ice only about 1 to 20 km across, too small to be resolved by telescopes on earth

<u>What is the relevance?</u>

to provide a complete description of a comet head

Page Number	Exercise Number	Answers (and Comments)
24	1	**What is the topic?** photometry **What is the class?** a measurement system in the field of astronomy **What is the description?** measurement of the brightness of astronomical objects by electronic devices (*specific description is provided in passage—for example, "the basic device is a photomultiplier . . ."*) **What is the relevance?** allows astronomers to measure temperature, composition, and other properties of a remote astronomical object
25	2	**What are three additional questions answered by the passage?** Sample questions: —How was measurement done previously? —How does a photomultiplier work? —Are there other uses for the technique?
26	1	**What is the topic?** planetology **What is the class?** This excerpt does not directly name the class other than to state that it is a field of study regarding planets. **What is the description?** the study of individual planets and systems of planets; the study, for example, of surfaces, atmospheres, interiors, and evolution

Page Number	Exercise Number	Answers (and Comments)

What is the relevance?

Since this topic pertains to the "study of" planets, one of the purposes would be to gain more information about planets. The excerpt does not tell us what its role is in the larger context of the chapter.

| 26 | 2 | |

What is the topic?

comparative planetology

What is the class?

a type of planetology; an *approach* to studying planets

What is the description?

a study of how planets compare with one another, why they are different, and why certain planets have certain similarities.

What is the relevance?

to be able to compare planets, rather than considering them in isolation as traditional planetology did

| 26 | 3 | |

What is one other question answered by the passage?

Sample questions:

—What equipment has led to the new approach?

—What is an example of the approach taken in comparative planetology?

Your definition may look something like this (remember: this is just an example):

Page Number	**Exercise Number**	**Answers (and Comments)**
28		*Filtration is a physical process used to separate mixtures into individual substances. It consists of pouring a mixture in which one of the substances is already liquid or has been dissolved to become liquid through a filter; this results in the liquid draining through the filter and the solid substance being caught by the filter.*

The important point is this: does your answer contain the following information? That is, does it answer these questions?

What is the topic?

filtration

What is the class?

a physical process (for separating mixtures)

What is the description?

It consists of pouring a mixture. (See sample answer.)

What is the relevance?

It is used to separate and purify mixtures.

| 28 | | "What is distillation?" |

Somewhere in your answer or definition the following information should appear.

What is the topic?

distillation

What is the class?

a physical process

Page Number	Exercise Number	Answers (and Comments)

What is the <u>description?</u>

It consists of boiling liquid mixtures, then collecting and condensing the vapors of the individual substances, which vaporize at different temperatures. Repeating the process increases the purity of the individual substances.

What is the <u>relevance?</u>

Is it used to separate and purify mixtures.

29

Your definition of *psychoanalysis* should include the following information, however or wherever it may be expressed:

What is the <u>topic?</u>
psychoanalysis

What is the <u>class?</u>
a method of psychotherapy

What is the <u>description?</u>
The method seeks to bring unconscious material to consciousness in clients through the use of such techniques as: free association, dream analysis, and transference.

What is the <u>relevance?</u>
It is used to try to help clients achieve insight into why they do what they do and think what they think.

29

Your definition of *catharsis* should include the following information, no matter how you choose to express it:

What is the <u>topic?</u>
catharsis

Page Number	Exercise Number	Answers (and Comments)

What is the <u>class?</u>

process

What is the <u>description?</u>

the release of pent-up emotions while unconscious thought processes are brought to consciousness

What is the <u>relevance?</u>

There is no other information beyond what is stated in the description.

30

Your definition of *free association* should include the following information, however or wherever it may be expressed:

What is the <u>topic?</u>

free association

What is the <u>class?</u>

a method used in psychoanalysis

What is the <u>description?</u>

The client lies on the couch, starts thinking about a particular symptom or problem, and then reports everything that comes to mind—a word, phrase, visual image. The client is not to omit anything, censor anything, or to worry about expressing thoughts in complete sentences. The therapist then processes and analyzes this information.

What is the <u>relevance?</u>

The last two lines of the excerpt begin to tell us, the readers, what the use of this method is. We can easily infer that the therapist will use the information in order to analyze the client's problem.

Page Number	**Exercise Number**	**Answers (and Comments)**

31

Sample answer:

"Fascism is an ideology that asserts the supremacy of the nation or race over the interest of individuals or groups. It perceives the state as not merely a governmental bureaucracy but the organic life of a whole people."

The excerpt does not make any specific reference to relevance. The other three questions are answered.

31–37

No answer keys are provided for the five exercises on these pages since in some instances there is no one correct answer in terms of which exact words should be marked by an underline or a wavy line. The main purpose of the exercises is that you become even more aware about the different types of information you are finding—or not finding—as you read. After you have marked each passage we suggest that you

- review your own marking to see if, for example, the underlined words really do describe the topic rather than tell about its relevance or impact. Do they answer the questions: "What is x?" and not "What is x useful for?" and not "What impact does x have?"

- compare with a classmate how each of you marked the passages. Even if you have different opinions about some parts of a passage, you will refine your understanding of description and relevance as you discuss them.

37

Topic: automatic stabilizers

Page Number	Exercise Number	Answers (and Comments)
		Class: Government programs (thus stabilizers are a type of program)
38		Description: This information is provided by two examples of how two automatic stabilizers work; these two are income taxes and welfare programs. There is no general description of the characteristics.
		Relevance: They are designed to counter the effects of economic cycles (and thus provide economic stability).
39		No answer key is provided for this exercise since in some instances there is no one correct answer in terms of which exact words should be marked by an underline or a wavy line. The main purpose of the exercises is that you become even more aware about the different types of information you are finding— or not finding—as you read. After you have marked each passage we suggest that you

- review your own marking to see if, for example, the underlined words really do describe the topic rather than tell about its relevance or impact. Do they answer the question: "What is x?" and not "What is x useful for?" and not "What impact does x have?"

- compare with a classmate how each of you marked the passages. Even if you have different opinions about some parts of a passage, you will refine your understanding of description and relevance as you discuss them.

Page Numbers	Credits
21, 36, 37	Thomas R. Dye, *Power and Society,* 5th ed., © 1990 by Harcourt Brace and Company. Reprinted by permission of the publisher.
23, 24, 25	William K. Hartman and Chris Impey, *Astronomy: The Cosmic Journey,* 5th ed., © 1994 by Wadsworth, Inc. Used by permission of the publisher.
27–28	G. Tyler Miller, Jr., *Chemistry: A Basic Introduction,* 4th ed., © 1987 Wadsworth, Inc.
29, 31–32, 34, 35, 60–65	James W. Kalat, *Introduction to Psychology.* Copyright 1996, 1993, 1990, 1986 Wadsworth Publishing Company. Used by permission of Brooks/Cole Publishing Company, Pacific Grove, CA, a division of International Thomson Publishing Inc.
39	Andrew Cohen, *Language Learning,* 1990, Heinle and Heinle Publishers.